# Lone-Parent Families

## ISSUES

## Volume 75

Editor

Craig Donnellan

*Independence*

Educational Publishers
Cambridge

First published by Independence
PO Box 295
Cambridge CB1 3XP
England

**British Library Cataloguing in Publication Data**
Lone-Parent Families – (Issues Series)
I. Donnellan, Craig II. Series
306.8'56'0941

ISBN 1 86168 264 6

**Printed in Great Britain**
MWL Print Group Ltd

**Typeset by**
Claire Boyd

**Cover**
The illustration on the front cover is by
Pumpkin House.

# CONTENTS

# Introduction

*Lone-Parent Families* is the seventy-fifth volume in the **Issues** series. The aim of this series is to offer up-to-date information about important issues in our world.

*Lone-Parent Families* looks at teenage parenthood and one-parent families.

The information comes from a wide variety of sources and includes:
Government reports and statistics
Newspaper reports and features
Magazine articles and surveys
Web site material
Literature from lobby groups
and charitable organisations.

It is hoped that, as you read about the many aspects of the issues explored in this book, you will critically evaluate the information presented. It is important that you decide whether you are being presented with facts or opinions. Does the writer give a biased or an unbiased report? If an opinion is being expressed, do you agree with the writer?

*Lone-Parent Families* offers a useful starting-point for those who need convenient access to information about the many issues involved. However, it is only a starting-point. At the back of the book is a list of organisations which you may want to contact for further information.

*****

# Teenage pregnancy and parenthood

## Information from the Health Development Agency

### Introduction

It is widely understood that teenage pregnancy and early motherhood can be associated with poor educational achievement, poor physical and mental health, social isolation, poverty and related factors. There is also a growing recognition that socio-economic disadvantage can be both a cause and a consequence of teenage parenthood.

### Teenage pregnancy and parenthood in the UK

The UK has the highest rate of teenage pregnancies in western Europe. Throughout most of the region, birth rates to teenage mothers fell during the 1970s, but UK rates have been fairly consistent, staying relatively stable since 1969. Between 1998 and 2000, the under-18 and under-16 conception rates have fallen by over 6%, and:

- In 2000, 38,690 under-18-year-olds in England became pregnant
- 44.8% of these ended in legal abortion
- 7,617 of these conceptions were to under-16s
- 54.5% of conceptions to under-16s ended in legal abortion.

In 1998, the Social Exclusion Unit (SEU) was asked by the Prime Minister to study the causes of teenage pregnancy and to develop a strategy to reduce the high rates of teenage pregnancy and parenthood in England. The SEU published its report, *Teenage Pregnancy*, and this provides a comprehensive review of the area and identifies the most effective approaches to tackle teenage pregnancy.

The main aims of the national strategy are to:

- Reduce the rate of teenage conceptions, with the specific aim of halving the rate of conceptions among under-18-year-olds by 2010. *The NHS Plan* provides a target for an interim reduction of 15% by 2004
- Set a firmly established downward trend in the under-16 conception rates by 2010
- Reduce inequality in rates between the 20% of wards with the highest rate of teenage conception and the average wards by at least 25%
- Increase to 60% the participation of teenage parents in education, training and employment to reduce their risk of long-term social exclusion by 2010.

That report sets out a ten-year national strategy for meeting these aims, and a concerted programme of

---

*The UK has the highest rate of teenage pregnancies in western Europe*

---

national and regional work, co-ordinated by the cross-government Teenage Pregnancy Unit (TPU), is under way.

### Who becomes a teenage parent?

Girls and young women from social class V are at approximately ten times the risk of becoming teenage mothers as girls and young women from social class I. Young people with below average achievement levels at ages 7 and 16 have also been found to be at significantly higher risk of becoming teenage parents.

We know less about who becomes a young father (but the above refers to young parents). Evidence suggests that young fathers (defined as those who became fathers before the age of 22), like young mothers, are more likely to come from lower socio-economic groups, from families that have experienced financial difficulties, and are more likely than average to have left school at the minimum age.

There is some evidence that certain groups of young people seem

to be particularly vulnerable to becoming teenage parents. They include:

- Young people in or leaving care
- Homeless young people
- School excludees, truants and young people under-performing at school
- Children of teenage mothers
- Members of some ethnic minority groups – for example, Caribbean, Pakistani and Bangladeshi women are more likely than white women to have been teenage mothers
- Young people involved in crime
- Conception rates are slightly higher in the north of England than the south, although there is a lot of regional variation.

### What happens to teenage parents and their children?

Although parenthood can be a positive and life-enhancing experience for some young people, it may also bring a number of negative consequences for young parents and their children. These factors include:

- Negative short-, medium- and long-term health and mental health outcomes for young mothers

- Education and employment – as well as being more likely to have problems at school before they become pregnant, young mothers are less likely to complete their education, have no qualifications by age 33, be in receipt of benefits and if employed be on lower incomes than their peers
- Housing – 80% of under-18 mothers live in someone else's household (e.g. parents), and teenagers are more likely to have to move house during pregnancy
- Family – teenage mothers are more likely to be lone parents, and more likely to find themselves in the middle of family conflict
- Young fathers – although there is little data on this group, health, economic and employment outcomes for young fathers post-parenthood seem to be similar to those of young mothers.

There may also be negative outcomes for the babies and children of teenage mothers:

- Babies tend to have a lower than average birth weight
- Infant mortality in this group is 60% higher than for babies of older women
- Some 44% of mothers under 20

breastfeed, compared to 64% of 20- 24-year-olds and up to 80% of older mothers
- Children of teenage mothers are more likely to have the experience of being a lone-parent family, and are generally at increased risk of poverty, poor housing and having bad nutrition
- Daughters of teenage mothers may be more likely to become teenage parents themselves.

■ This briefing presents the current evidence from selected systematic and other reviews and meta-analyses published since 1996. The full review – Swann, C., Bowe,K., McCormick, G., Kosmin, M. (2003) *Teenage pregnancy and parenthood: a review of reviews.* London: HDA – will be updated regularly as new evidence becomes available. It can be accessed via: www.hda-online.org.uk/evidence It seeks to pull together learning from review-level data about effective interventions to reduce the rates of teenage pregnancy and improve the outcomes for teenage parents.

*© Health Development Agency 2003.*
*Available online at: www.hda.nhs.uk/evidence*

# *Teenage pregnancy*

## Information from fpa

The UK has the highest teenage pregnancy rate in Western Europe. fpa wishes to see this rate reduced because evidence shows that teenage mothers and their children are more likely to experience a range of long-term negative educational, social, health and economic outcomes. However, fpa recognises that every young woman is an individual, living in a unique set of circumstances, with a right to make her own sexual and reproductive choices.

Every young women should have the freedom and capacity to choose whether to be sexually active, use contraception or become pregnant and, if pregnant, whether to continue with the pregnancy.

However, many young people in the UK lack the knowledge and skills to make these decisions and do not have access to services that will adequately support them.

School-based SRE has to-date been too little, too late and too biological. Teachers have been poorly trained and boys have felt excluded by the emphasis on the reproductive process. The Sex

Education Forum states 'Sex and relationships education is lifelong learning about sex, sexuality, emotions, relationships and sexual health.' SRE should be mandatory, provided by trained teachers and place the needs of the child firmly at its centre. Support should also be available for parents to enable them to talk with their children about sex.

All young people must have access to services that will provide information about sexual health and a range of contraceptive choices. They must be acceptable to all young people, open at appropriate times, offer and publicise confidentiality and the staff must be trained to understand the needs of young

## Teenage conception rates

| England and Wales | | | | | | | | | Rates per 1,000 conceptions | |
|---|---|---|---|---|---|---|---|---|---|---|
| | Leading to maternities | | | | | Leading to abortion | | | | |
| | 1971 | 1981 | 1991 | 1996 | 1999 | 1971 | 1981 | 1991 | 1996 | 1999 |
| **Age at conception** | | | | | | | | | | |
| Under 14[1] | 0.5 | 0.4 | 0.5 | 0.6 | 0.5 | 0.5 | 0.7 | 0.7 | 0.8 | 0.7 |
| 14 | 2.8 | 1.7 | 2.6 | 2.7 | 2.4 | 2.4 | 2.9 | 3.6 | 3.6 | 3.3 |
| 15 | 12.5 | 7.1 | 9.8 | 11.0 | 9.0 | 6.9 | 8.7 | 9.3 | 9.4 | 9.2 |
| All aged under 16[1] | 5.5 | 3.1 | 4.3 | 4.8 | 3.9 | 3.2 | 4.1 | 4.6 | 4.7 | 4.4 |
| 16 | 41.0 | 21.5 | 25.0 | 27.1 | 24.0 | 13.0 | 16.2 | 17.1 | 17.9 | 18.8 |
| 17 | 68.5 | 36.7 | 41.5 | 42.5 | 40.8 | 15.2 | 20.1 | 22.7 | 24.1 | 25.9 |
| 18 | 95.0 | 54.6 | 57.0 | 56.5 | 53.5 | 16.7 | 21.6 | 26.6 | 29.2 | 30.3 |
| 19 | 114.5 | 73.0 | 66.2 | 66.5 | 61.6 | 16.4 | 21.0 | 28.6 | 31.4 | 32.4 |
| All aged under 20[1] | 67.3 | 38.9 | 42.0 | 40.4 | 38.6 | 14.3 | 18.2 | 22.1 | 23.0 | 24.3 |

1 Rates for girls aged under 14, under 16 and under 20 are based on population of girls aged 13, 13 to 15 and 15 to 19, respectively.

women and young men, including the under-16-year-olds. Carers, professionals and providers should ensure that young people know how to access these services.

Clear accurate information and access to emergency contraception (EC) should be more easily available to young people. EC should be free of charge and available from a choice of providers in or near to places where young people spend most of their time, e.g. schools. Staff must be trained to issue EC without making young people feel reprimanded or belittled.

*All young people must have access to services that will provide information about sexual health and a range of contraceptive choices*

The decision to have an abortion rests with the woman herself whatever her age; abortion access and treatment should be based on this principle. However, children in the UK grow up in a culture that is biased and ill informed about abortion. SRE and health services should present abortion as a valid option and provide accurate information for boys and girls. Young women should have access to free non-directive pregnancy counselling and supportive, timely services.

Sexually explicit media images may give an impression of UK society as being at ease with sexuality but this is not the case. Teenage sexuality, in particular, is viewed in a negative light and young people's sexual activity seen as sexual deviance or promiscuity. Pregnancy in teenage girls indicates that they are sexually active leading to scapegoating by the media and pressure groups. The well-being of the young women, their partners and children should always be the primary concern.

Programmes to reduce the teenage pregnancy rate should not cause pregnant teenagers to be seen as bad or stupid because stigmatisation will have long-term detrimental consequences for both the young parents and their children. A balance must be sought between enabling young people to avoid pregnancy while supporting young women who do become pregnant and young fathers.

fpa is primarily concerned with the sexual health aspects of teenage pregnancy but it is recognised that where young people have ambition and expectations, rates of teenage pregnancy are low. Many young women in the UK live in communities where teenage pregnancy is the norm and to have a child early is seen as a way of achieving something positive in life. Social inequalities must be addressed in order to secure real freedom of choice for all young people.

■ The above information is from fpa's web site which can be found at www.fpa.org.uk

© fpa

*fpa* believes that teenagers should be in the position to decide whether or not to have a child and that this must be a fully informed, supported choice.

*fpa* believes that all children should learn how to prevent pregnancy as part of sex and relationships education (SRE) beginning before puberty and based on the acquisition of knowledge, skills and positive attitudes about sexuality.

*fpa* believes that sexual and primary care services that are confidential and acceptable should be accessible to all young people.

*fpa* believes that all young people should have accurate information about emergency contraception and how to access it quickly and easily.

*fpa* believes that good SRE presents abortion as a valid option and that young women must have easy access to supportive counselling and abortion services.

*fpa* believes that much of the moral outrage focused on teenage mothers involves unease about teenage sexuality and this should not be allowed to cloud what should be a young-person-centred issue.

*fpa* believes that there must be no stigmatisation of pregnant teenagers and that teenage mothers and fathers should be fully supported.

*fpa* believes that the range of cultural and socio-economic factors which underlie teenage pregnancy rates must be addressed for rates to be reduced.

# Teenage conceptions

## Statistics and trends

### Teenage conceptions

#### Under-20s
In 2001[a], 60.9 in every 1,000 15-19-year-olds became pregnant in England and Wales.[1] In Scotland, in 2001, the rate per 1,000 16-19-year-olds was 70.6.[2]

#### Under-16s
In 2001, 8 in every 1,000 13-15-year-olds became pregnant in England and Wales.[1] In Scotland, in 2001, the rate for the same age group was 7.6.[2]

### Outcome of teenage pregnancy

#### Abortions
The likelihood of a pregnant teenager having an abortion decreases with age. 61% of 14-year-olds have abortions; among 15-year-olds the figure is 54%, at 17, 42% and at 19, 35% (England & Wales 2001).

#### Births
In 2001 around 22,200 under-18-year-olds gave birth in England and Wales – a rate of 23.1 per 1,000.[1] In Northern Ireland in 2001, the number of teenage mothers was 1,524[3] – a rate of 23.9 per 1,000.[b]

In Scotland, 5,166 16-19-year-olds gave birth in 2001– a rate of 41.5 per 1,000.[2]

### Teenage pregnancy – is the trend up or down?
Teenagers are far less likely to get pregnant today than they were in the early 1970s. The conception rate in 1970 was 82.4 per 1,000 15-19-year-olds compared with 60.9 in 2001.[c]

The decline in teenage mothers is even more striking. In 1970, 71.4 per 1,000 15-19-year-olds had a baby, almost twice the rate in 2001. The proportion of pregnant teenagers choosing motherhood declined sharply after the 1967 Abortion Act offered young people the choice of terminating an unwanted pregnancy.

### Teenage pregnancy – the trends over the last 25 years
After the introduction of free contraception on the NHS in 1975, teenage conception rates for the 15-19 age group steadily declined, reaching the lowest recorded figure in 1983.

Later in the 1980s that downward trend reversed. Between 1983 and 1990 the rate rose by 23%. Rates fell again in the early 1990s but rose between 1995 and 1998. Since 1998 the teenage conception rate has started to decline, falling overall by 7%.

The conception rate for 13-15-year-olds has followed much the same pattern as for older teenagers, but usually with less marked variation. Since 1998, however, the conception rate for under-16s has fallen by 11%.

Between 1998 and 2001 there was also a fall of almost 10% in conception rates amongst under-18s from 47 per thousand to 42.5 per thousand.[1]

### What caused the teenage conception rate to rise in the 1980s?

#### Fears over confidentiality
Research has shown consistently that young people will not use services

unless they are sure that they are confidential. It is Brook's experience that controversy in the 1980s around the question of providing contraception confidentially to under-16s confused many of their clients over the right to advice and may have deterred many young people from visiting contraceptive services. Attendance figures for under-16s at Brook and family planning clinics in England showed a significant drop during this period. Although the legal issues surrounding confidentiality and under 16s were resolved in the House of Lords in 1985 in favour of young people's rights, attendance figures for this age group did not recover until 1990.[4]

#### Cuts in services
Funding cuts in community health services forced the closure of many family planning and young people's services, restricting access to help.

#### Unemployment and youth opportunities
The effect of the recession increased youth unemployment, undermining young people's motivation to delay having a baby.

### . . . and fall in the 1990s?
In England and Wales, between 1990 and 1995, there was a 15% reduction in the conception rate among 15-19-year-olds and a 16% decline amongst under-16s. This coincided with an expansion of young people's services from 52% of health authorities providing a specialist service in 1990 to over 85% in 1995. This downward trend was reversed in 1996.

#### The impact of the 1995 pill alert
In 1996, teenage conception rates in England and Wales rose significantly. This followed the pill alert in 1995 about the apparent increased risk of venous thromboembolism in 'third generation' pills. The percentage of Brook clients choosing the pill in

1996 dropped by 32% among the under-16s and 25% among 16-19-year-olds.[5]

## Factors associated with teenage parenthood[6]

*Low educational attainment*
Low educational attainment is the most powerful single factor associated with becoming a young parent.

*Poverty*
Teenage parents are more likely to come from families with low socio-economic status and financial hardship.

*Emotional difficulties*
Young parents, particularly teenage mothers, are much more likely to have a history of serious behaviour problems.

*Being a child of a teenage mother*
26% of young mothers and 22% of young fathers had teenage mothers compared with 13% of women and men who became parents at a later age.

## Regional variations in teenage pregnancy rates

Teenage conception rates vary widely across the country. In 2001, South East London Health Authority had a conception rate of 89.2 per thousand 15-19-year-olds, compared with a rate of 43.8 in Surrey and Sussex.

The teenage conception rate is considerably higher in deprived areas of the country compared with affluent areas. However, pregnant teenagers in more affluent areas are more likely to choose abortion.[7]

## Teenage mothers and single parents

Although teenagers are far less likely to have a baby today compared with 20 years ago, they are more likely to have the baby outside marriage. This reflects the trend away from the 'shotgun marriage' which carried a high risk of divorce, towards cohabitation. In 1995, 67% of babies born to teenagers outside marriage were jointly registered with both parents. In 1995, 59% of the parents were resident at the same address.

However, teenagers make up only a small proportion of single parents. The proportion of births

*26% of young mothers and 22% of young fathers had teenage mothers compared with 13% of women and men who became parents at a later age*

outside marriage born to teenagers has decreased from 1971 to 1990 from 39% to 28%.

## International comparisons

*Factors associated with low teenage pregnancy rates*[8]
- An open and accepting attitude to teenage sexuality.
- Widely available information and sex education.
- Easy access to confidential contraceptive services.

The Netherlands has the lowest teenage conception rate of developed countries – one-sixth of that in the United Kingdom. Comparable conception data are not available from other European countries. However, in an international comparison of teenage birth rates, the United Kingdom topped the European league.

*Footnotes*
a  Latest available figures.
b  Conception data not collected in Northern Ireland because no abortions are recorded. The only available statistics are for teenage births.
c  England and Wales only. Comparable data over the same period of time are not available for Scotland or Northern Ireland.

*References*
1  *Health Statistics Quarterly*, 17. National Statistics, Spring 2003
2  Information and Statistics Division Website, Scottish Health Service. Provisional figures
3  Northern Ireland Registrar General's Annual Report 2001
4  *NHS Contraceptive Services, England: 1997-98.* Department of Health
5  Brook Advisory Centres Annual Report 1996-97
6  Social Backgrounds and post-birth experiences of young parents. Joseph Rowntree Foundation. *Social Policy Research 80.* July 1995
7  Influence of socio-economic factors on attaining targets. T. Smith, *British Medical Journal*, 306, 1993
8  Teenage Pregnancy in Developed Countries: Determinants and policy implications. E. Jones et al. *Family Planning Perspectives*, Vol. 17, March/April 1995

■ The above information is from Brook. See page 41 for their address details.

# Junior jury: teen pregnancy

**Are teenagers too young to have children? What do their peers think of them? Young people discuss the pros and cons of teenage pregnancy with *Children's Express* reporters**

'If someone young in my family did get pregnant I don't think it would really affect me because it would be their choice. But if they were under-age I would think they were just being stupid. People should wait 'til they are around 21 when they are a proper adult before they get pregnant, although if teenagers don't want to have an abortion then they shouldn't be forced to. The right age to have a child is around 20/21. I might be ready to have a baby in my twenties or early thirties.'

Claire Dennis, 12,
Cowgate

'I don't think that teenage girls should be pregnant under the age of 16 because it's unfair boys getting them like that when they don't want to have sex. Nobody under-age has been pregnant in my family. If someone in my family did get pregnant I think I would be very upset and my parents would flip.

I don't think the legal age to have a child is too young because people want to start a new life away from their parents and all that. Telling young people when they can and can't have children does not make them want to do it more because teenagers should have sex over 16. Parents should stick by their child because no matter what, that person is theirs. I think the right age to have a child is in the twenties.'

Michael Holland, 11,
Blakelaw

'A teenager really shouldn't have kids because it's wasting their lives, plus they don't have the maturity or other parent stuff needed because they are still kids themselves. I would be able to cope if either myself or someone close became pregnant

because I think I am a bit more mature than half the other kids that have bairns, although in another respect, no, because I would not have the money for a child to give it security and clothes and that.

They shouldn't have an age limit on sex basically, because no matter what, people are having it. You can be mature enough to have a baby at a young age but my ideal age would be 22, because you have got to have your life basically before you have kids. I don't think I will ever be emotionally ready to have a baby. If young people discussed having a baby with their family before they slept together they could be advised by the parents on whether to use condoms or the pill.'

Lindsay Marchant, 18,
Cowgate

---

**'Young people should be taught more about contraception in schools and in youth clubs to try and prevent teenage pregnancy'**

'Young people should be taught more about contraception in schools and in youth clubs to try and prevent teenage pregnancy. Also, I think it's wrong because it's babies having babies. I don't think I could cope if I fell pregnant, as I am not mature enough to have a child, even though I have been in a long-term relationship and my boyfriend would support me. If I did fall pregnant I would be lucky to have my boyfriend stand by me because most boys would get a girl pregnant and they wouldn't want anything to do with her.

Most kids are having sex when they are 11 and 12 years old and that is far too young because they don't know what they are letting themselves in for. I don't think there is a perfect age to have a baby. As long as you are mature enough and can afford to give a child the best life. In fact, you can vote when you're 18, so why is it wrong to be a teenage mother at 18? I think girls over the age of 12 should be on the pill because they are starting to think about sex so I think they should be prepared and protected. I think I will be ready to have a baby when I am 21 or above.'

Amy Wood, 18,
Cowgate

### About the team

Editor: Zoe Marchant, 15. Reporters: Claire Riley, 14, and Kirsten Caine, 12. Children's Express Newcastle is a programme of learning through journalism for young people eight to 18, run in partnership with Save the Children. Their web site is www.childrens-express.org/newcastle Junior Jury is a weekly column published in the *Newcastle Evening Chronicle*.

# 'People are constantly judging us'

**Three teenage mothers tell their stories to Thomas Vipond, who knows a thing or two about the subject – his mother is only 17 years older than him**

People tend to look at me strangely when I am introduced as my mother's son. Sometimes they find it impossible to hide their disbelief and say 'No' several times with increasing degrees of astonishment. This is usually followed by: 'But he's so big.' They then look my mum up and down as if to say: 'How did this 6ft 2in chubby monster come out of you?'

My mother is 33 and I am 16. She was my age when she gave birth to me and going through everything I am now – GCSEs and wondering what she wanted to do in life – but she had a baby to look after too. I can't imagine how difficult that was. The only blessing was that she had a very supportive family who helped her every step along the way. It wasn't always easy: financially, things have been always been pretty tight. When my mum went to university, we didn't have much money at all. I was there from the age of two to six and I spent most of my young days in the university crèche. (I feel as if I've already been to university – and it was rubbish.)

One of the worst things about having a young mother is that sometimes people assume, because I'm big and she's young, that I am her boyfriend – albeit a bit of a toyboy. Once, on a visit to Ireland a couple of years ago, we stopped at a tourist information centre in Boyle and had a chat with the lady working there. At first it was fine – she told us about the local history and tourist attractions, places to stay, and I found it interesting and informative. But then she suddenly veered off into dangerous territory, telling us about a lovely little place called Lovers' Island. I sensed what was coming

---

*One of the worst things about having a young mother is that sometimes people assume, because I'm big and she's young, that I am her boyfriend – albeit a bit of a toyboy*

---

and looked at the door. It wasn't far and I thought I could make it. I sprang like a puma, but before I could reach the salvation of outside, she said, with a grin and a wink: 'It's very romantic.' This was too embarrassing for a then very self-conscious teenager: I ran to the nearest body of cool water and threw myself in, hoping to wash away my mortification. My mum thought it was all very funny. Needless to say, I didn't, and for the rest of the journey I maintained a certain distance from her.

That was one of my worst experiences of having a young mother. It has been difficult, but nowadays I think it's great. I think I have a really good relationship with my mum: it's a very open one and I can talk to her about most things. She – dare I say it – is kind of cool. She knows what's happening out there – well, sort of.

But even though things are great now, and in general people have become accustomed to our situation, there was a time when my mum only encountered negativity about our

situation. Once a teacher in my mum's school summed her up with the words: 'Well, she's made her bed . . .' Attitudes like that really annoy me. Highly judgemental and lacking in compassion, they only serve to make young mothers more insecure and thus conform to the stereotypical image of them. My mother only experienced a little bit of this treatment; fortunately for her, it made her determined to succeed.

However, I wanted to find out how the prejudices and stigma attached to teenage pregnancy affect young mothers today. I arranged to meet three at a project in Oldham, run by Brook, in partnership with Lifelong learning. The young mothers there work as volunteers, delivering peer-education programmes. They hold interactive sessions at schools, where they look at the roles and responsibilities of teenage parents and the difficulties and prejudices they still face.

Lynsey Tullin is 17. 'I feel people are constantly judging me,' she says. 'They look at me as an unfit mother if my baby starts crying.' To her great credit, Tullin is all the more determined to prove these people wrong. But why should she have to be determined to succeed? Is it only the determined ones that do? Does the system help young mothers who aren't as self-confident?

All three women feel let down by the financial assistance they receive from the government. Jackie Slater is 18: 'I hardly receive enough money to get by on. The only help I feel I've received is from charities like the Threshold housing project,' she says.

Why do these women feel so let down by the government? They need as much help as any mother does – perhaps more, as they are so young. Gemma Swan, who is an 18-year-old mother of three, has come through a very difficult situation and triumphed. She now helps other young people understand the situation she was in – Swan experienced prejudice from the people you would expect to help her the most. 'Health visitors and nurses were very judging and unkind to me when I was having my first child,' she says.

All three women agreed that things aren't going to change drastically in the near future. Some teenagers are still going to get pregnant, no matter what education they receive. However, they obviously feel that people's ideas and attitudes have to change.

---

*'I feel people are constantly judging me, they look at me as an unfit mother if my baby starts crying'*

---

I feel a lot more confident about the future of young mothers knowing that the three young women I talked to are helping and educating other young people with their experiences. All three agreed that they thought their programme got a better response than anything that was available to them when they were at school. For the young people they are talking to, there cannot be anything more powerful and relevant than someone who speaks from their own experience.

I am so impressed with this project. These young women are working intelligently to make a better future for themselves and their children. They are also helping other young people to form ideas about their future. Tullin, Slater and Swan have certainly not made their beds.

This summer, I am going to be making choices: what A-levels I am going to take; what I am going to do when I leave school. All teenagers are making choices, which involve more responsibility and independence. I hope that when I come to make these decisions, I receive the support and encouragement I need. Young people need it for all the choices they make – and that includes choosing to go through with pregnancy.

■ To contact the Brook Helpline for Young People, call 0800 0185 023, or visit www.brook.org.uk. In the Oldham area, contact oldhambrook@aol.com

■ This article first appeared in *The Guardian*, 7 July, 2003.

© *Thomas Vipond*

# The problems of parenthood

Being a teenage parent is not at all easy. Parenting is a long and difficult process and not many teenage mothers think they have the skills to do it well. This is not to say that very young parents always get it wrong, but it is almost always a hard and lonely struggle. It's often difficult for a teenage mother (usually the one left holding the baby) to complete her education and this affects her chances of getting a job and earning enough money to live on later on.

Teenage fathers are often left out of the picture all together. All the publicity about teenage pregnancy seems to focus on the girl rather than the boy. There is a feeling that somehow it's all the girl's fault, she should have known better. So, little is done to educate boys that they also have rights, responsibilities and choices about sex and pregnancy. Who knows how many more young teenage fathers would choose to stay with their child and partner if they had more support?

You would think that a good place to discuss these sorts of ideas and choices would be in sex education lessons at school – as well as in the home. However, boys often say they feel left out of sex education because so much attention is focused on pregnancy.

Go to the Sex Education Forum at the National Children's Bureau website and see if you can find the Young People's Charter for Sex and Relationships Education.

■ The above information is from Barnardo's web site which can be found at www.barnardos.org.uk

© *Barnardo's*

# Teenage pregnancy

## Information from www.youthinformation.com

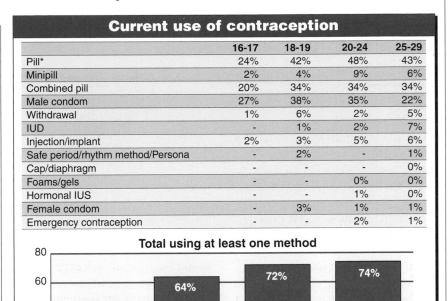

**Current use of contraception**

| | 16-17 | 18-19 | 20-24 | 25-29 |
|---|---|---|---|---|
| Pill* | 24% | 42% | 48% | 43% |
| Minipill | 2% | 4% | 9% | 6% |
| Combined pill | 20% | 34% | 34% | 34% |
| Male condom | 27% | 38% | 35% | 22% |
| Withdrawal | 1% | 6% | 2% | 5% |
| IUD | - | 1% | 2% | 7% |
| Injection/implant | 2% | 3% | 5% | 6% |
| Safe period/rhythm method/Persona | - | 2% | - | 1% |
| Cap/diaphragm | - | - | - | 0% |
| Foams/gels | - | - | 0% | 0% |
| Hormonal IUS | - | - | 1% | 0% |
| Female condom | - | 3% | 1% | 1% |
| Emergency contraception | - | - | 2% | 1% |

**Total using at least one method**

- 16-17: 39%
- 18-19: 64%
- 20-24: 72%
- 25-29: 74%

\* Includes women who did not know the type of pill used.

Source: Crown copyright

Britain has the highest rate of teenage pregnancy in Europe. The Government is keen to address this alarming trend. The Social Exclusion Unit published their report in June 1999 on teenage pregnancy.

The SEU aims to halve the rates of teenage pregnancies over the next ten years, and to lessen the risks of young parents suffering the consequences of social exclusion. They intend to do this by getting more teenage parents back into education, training or employment. The report forms the basis of a new £60 million national programme to tackle the causes and effects of teenage pregnancy.

As a result of the report a national publicity campaign is planned to raise awareness among young people. It will:

- tell young people how hard it is to be a parent, and how easy it is to get pregnant;
- encourage young men to resist peer pressure to start having sex too young and to know the costs to their own health of having unprotected sex;
- ensure that the Child Support Agency leaves them in no doubt of their financial obligations to support their children;
- offer advice and support for parents to help them talk to their children about sex and relationships;
- provide a helpline to advise teenagers on sex and relationships;
- introduce new guidance for the provision of contraceptives for under-16s and will set out the importance of counselling the young person about delaying their sexual activity;
- provide effective and accessible NHS contraceptive services for young men and women and improve the publicity assuring young people that they can talk to health professionals in confidence.

New guidance will also be issued to improve sex and relationships education within schools with an emphasis on ensuring young people resist pressure to have sex too early.

### Young people at risk

The report includes a section on 'at risk young people' in which it proposes that the Department of Health and the Department for Education and Employment will produce joint guidance for social workers and youth workers. The Social Exclusion Unit recommends that they can and should direct young people to seek advice and contraception if it appears that they are contemplating sexual activity or that they are already sexually active. The most vulnerable groups will be targeted too, including young people looked after by a local authority, those excluded from school and young offenders.

### Support for young mothers

Sure Start Plus schemes are based in areas already covered by both Sure Start and Health Action Zones. Mothers under 16 are required to return to education and 16- and 17-year-old parents will be able to take part in the Education Maintenance Allowance. This scheme applies to all 16- and 17-year-old mothers who cannot live with their parents or a partner. They are offered supervised semi-independent housing with support, not a tenancy on their own as previously offered by local councils.

The Government is also supporting new proposals to ensure that young mothers return to school after having a baby. The aim is to increase the support network for these young people and to encourage them to pursue their education.

### Pregnant and still at school

You have the right to an education until you are 19 years old. If you are under 16 your local education authority (LEA) has an obligation to provide you with education, whether you want it or not. If you are pregnant the same rules still apply.

■ The above information is from the web site www.youthinformation.com
© Youthinformation.com

# Poverty and young motherhood

## Link between poverty and young motherhood revealed

The YWCA is calling on the Government to step up its commitment to eradicate poverty and social exclusion of young parents, after a new study highlighted the strong links between poverty and teenage motherhood.

The report, *Poverty: The Price of Young Motherhood*, in Britain will be presented to a United Nations Commission in New York. The author of the report, the YWCA's Director of Policy and Campaigns, Mandana Hendessi, is urging people to stop demonising teenage mothers and puts forward a seven-point action plan to improve the plight of young parents in the UK, which still has the highest levels of teenage pregnancy and child poverty in western Europe.

The report includes a review of recent research and two separate studies carried out by the YWCA, comprising interviews with a total of 136 mothers in England and 26 agencies working with them. The interviews support recent research showing that poverty, low educational attainment and poor self-esteem combine to form a vicious circle for young women in the most deprived areas of the UK, where the highest rates of early motherhood occur. Above all, the social stigmatisation of teenage parenthood and lone motherhood, in particular, has led to teenage mothers shying away from essential services.

There are also worrying findings in the report about young women from Bangladeshi and Pakistani communities, showing that restrictive family and cultural values often lead to Asian women having limited access to health and social services.

Whilst Ms Hendessi's report welcomes existing government initiatives to tackle poverty and social exclusion in the UK, it calls for wider measures to help young women. She said: 'Britain is the fourth richest industrial nation and yet we still have the highest rate of teenage pregnancy and child poverty in western Europe. We must act now to eradicate poverty and social exclusion. Crucially, it is time to stop demonising young mums.

'Evidence has shown time and again that young women do not get pregnant to get housing and welfare benefits; most of them, in fact, don't know about welfare entitlements before they get pregnant.

'The public hysteria about teenage mothers is unjustified and contributes to negative attitudes sometimes held by health and social care professionals, ironically the very people whose job it is to help teenage mothers. Such attitudes deter young women from accessing services at times when they are especially in need of assistance.'

As part of its action plan, the YWCA is calling on the Government to:

- Tackle the poverty experienced by young adults by increasing the minimum wage for those aged 21 and under to the adult rate
- Establish courses for all health and social care professionals on the issues and needs of young parents
- Fund childcare provision at further education and higher education colleges to encourage enrolment by young mothers
- Challenge the social stigma surrounding teenage pregnancy and motherhood by publicising existing research which has resolutely dispelled the myths about teenage motherhood

Oxfam UK, who part-funded the research, welcomed the YWCA's report and recommendations. Oxfam Gender Adviser, Sue Smith, said:

'Teenage mothers are amongst the poorest and most vulnerable people in the UK. This research is a timely investigation of how early motherhood is a poverty trap for young women. It provides important insights into the lives of the young women interviewed and offers solutions that will help Oxfam and the YWCA in their anti-poverty work in Great Britain.'

YWCA projects in some of the most deprived areas of England and Wales are already helping young women break the cycle of poverty and lack of opportunity. The charity provides a wide range of services for disadvantaged young women, many of whom are already mothers in their teens. The YWCA has led the way in providing on-site childcare, so that young mothers excluded from school or who have failed to gain qualifications can attend training and get back into education or into work.

- *Poverty: The Price of Young Motherhood in Britain* by Mandana Hendessi and Frahana Rashid is published by the YWCA and supported by Oxfam UK. ISBN: 0-901862-11-8, priced £8.

> 'Teenage mothers are amongst the poorest and most vulnerable people in the UK'

# Supporting young mums

**What kind of support are young mums and mums-to-be getting from local agencies involved in the Kirklees area's teenage pregnancy strategy?**

The Sure Start project, run by Kirklees Early Years Service in partnership with Kirklees Primary Care Trust, is based at Thornhill and Overthorpe Junior and Infant Schools in North Kirklees. It provides parents with help and support to develop their children's health and wellbeing and, via links to other local organisations, improved access to other family services and educational opportunities. It also supports the local Teenage Pregnancy Partnership.

'Young people sometimes do make the choice to have a child. No one wants to deny them that right,' explains parent support worker Diane Graham.

'We just want to make sure they are armed with all the facts beforehand. Very few of the young mothers we deal with are aware of the services – or benefits – available to them and, as a result, are not getting all the help they need.'

Fiona, age 17, planned to have a baby. She gave birth to Emily six months ago and is bringing her up with her partner. Supported by Sure Start, she also hopes to go to Dewsbury College.

'My gran died in 2000 and it really made me think about what my priorities were. I decided that I did want to be a mum. But I was lucky that I was in a stable relationship and I knew that my mum would support me. It has been a huge event in my life, though – even more so than I thought it would be. It changes things for ever – and if that's not something you are prepared to face, you should not even consider having a baby.

'When I was at school, there did not seem to be that many people you could ask, generally, about sex. So it's up to you to sort it out yourself. Teenagers need to ask advice on contraception – not to be embarrassed – and to know their body.'

*By Steve Murphy*

Fiona's mother, Jane, 'went through every emotion possible – and more' when she found out Fiona was pregnant.

'To other parents, I would say make sure you know what your child wants and try to support them as much as you can. There are a lot of organisations that do provide help, but sometimes finding them is difficult. That's when you really need the support from someone close to you.'

> *'Young people sometimes do make the choice to have a child. No one wants to deny them that right'*

Sheridan, age 17, recently gave birth to baby Ethan. At first she didn't tell her mum that she was pregnant.

'I was six weeks gone when I found out I was pregnant – and I had no idea what to do. I told my best friend, but didn't tell my family for a while. I was not sure of their reaction. When I did tell my mum she said she already knew – and she has really stood by me.'

With the support of Sure Start, her mum and other family and friends, Sheridan has also decided to go to Dewsbury College, where she will study health and social care. She adds: 'I don't think that having a baby needs to be the end of your life or career. If you get the right sort of help there is plenty you can do.'

Two other partners working on the Kirklees teenage pregnancy initiative are the Kirklees Pathway Team and the Single Homeless Accommodation Project (SHAP).

The Pathway Team provides looked-after children who are leaving care with career guidance, health advice and help to find accommodation up until the age of 21 (or in some cases, 24) and its advisers often work with teenage mothers.

Like Sure Start's Graham, Pathway personal adviser Kathy Ryall stresses that the strategy aims to prevent unwanted pregnancies – not stop young people having children. 'It's about help, support and awareness. We need to work with young people, to care and educate them – and to help them realise their goals.'

SHAP housing support worker (single parents' service) Diane Tavernier points out: 'Many young mums have never had to think about things such as a tenancy agreement. They can be thrown into the deep end and left to their own devices – with no understanding of how things can go wrong. There are other simple things, like knowing whether they are entitled to housing benefit – and how they claim it. We try to help people find their way around the system and provide practical, short-term help for mum, dad and baby.'

'Most young mums feel they are missing out on things, but none regret having their babies,' adds SHAP worker Sue Lambatt. 'They do all

seem to have felt very isolated at times – and cut off from their rights. If they push for the benefits they are entitled to, they say they are made to feel like they are grabbing... They all wish the situation could be better, but people need to recognise that it is hard for them to get by and [that we should] do our best to support them.'

Mum-to-be Gemma, age 19, has been receiving help from SHAP in Huddersfield. Like the majority of teenage pregnancies, hers was not planned. She is temporarily separated from the father.

'I told my grandmother about the pregnancy first and she did not want me to tell my father. But in the end I did. At first he went mad. But then he calmed down and has been very supportive since.'

She says one of the biggest problems was trying to get a job. 'People just do not want to employ someone who is pregnant, so you end up claiming benefits. But the Benefits Agency give you a hard time – as though you are not trying to find work.'

Gemma has benefited from Pathway's Independent Living Skills course, which provides young people with help to develop basic skills like cooking, cleaning and budgeting. In addition, the agency helped her to find and furnish a house.

'It's helped me to feel more confident in bringing up the baby on my own. It's a really daunting prospect, but Pathway has put me in touch with people from different organisations who can help.'

Cassie, age 19, has a 14-month-old daughter, Lacie. She was doing a health and social care course at Dewsbury College when she found out she was pregnant – and hopes to return to her studies, although she has suffered poor health since giving birth.

'I had a very supportive family around me but it still was not an easy time. I was worried about the future – and what would happen after the birth. I would tell other people, though, not to hide from their situation. You have to face it. To talk to people and make your own decisions.

'SHAP have been really helpful. They've helped me with accommodation and with getting everything ready for the baby. Through them I've also been able to do part-time college courses, which means I've been able to continue my education.'

© Health Development Today, August/ September 2003. Issue 16, pages 14-15. Published by the Health Development Agency. Also available online at www.hda.nhs.uk

# Young fathers

## Information from Youthinformation.com

The role of fathers in family life is changing. Research has shown that fathers who actively involve themselves in their child's development have a very important role to play. This is also true for young fathers. But all too often young fathers receive little support or encouragement and their role is not acknowledged – they tend to be an 'invisible' group under-provided for and under-represented.

Society often views young fathers in a negative light. This leads them to feel undervalued, disregarded and excluded and this can lead them to withdraw from family life, losing their self-esteem, and can have a serious effect on their confidence.

Many young fathers want to be there for their partner and to be involved in the caring for and upbringing of their baby. These young fathers see their role as a long-term commitment. According to Fathers Direct, research has suggested that:

- Many young fathers want to become involved with their children right from the start, rather than waiting until the child is older.
- Many young fathers are denied access to their baby for reasons such as personal relationships with partners and families.
- Many young men find the transition to fatherhood confusing, they lack clear information and support from family and professionals, and this increases their sense of alienation from their baby.

### Parental responsibility

To enable young fathers to get the same legal status as their child's mother, they can apply for parental responsibility. If the mother agrees you will need to complete the form available from the Central Registry. You can also pick up a copy of the form at your local court.

However, if the mother does not agree you can apply for a Parental Responsibility order through the court. This costs about £80. You will fill in a form and then the court will send you papers. All of these must be copied for your child's mother. You will both make statements before the court hearing and they decide on your application.

'Parental Responsibility' ends when your child reaches the age of 18. If you child is adopted you parental responsibility also ends.

### Paid paternity leave

New fathers are now entitled to eight weeks' paid paternity leave if they have been with the same employer for one year or longer. The eight weeks must be used before the child's eighth birthday. The government is planning to introduce paid paternity leave for new fathers. It is likely that they will be offered two weeks' paid leave at £60.20 a week. This is the same level as statutory maternity pay.

© Youthinformation.com

# British teenagers talk

## Children's Express is a programme of learning through journalism for children aged eight to 18

The British Government's report into teenage pregnancy advocated a much more practical approach to contraception such as giving advice out at school. While parents may protest, teenagers themselves think contraception is crucial to reducing Britain's record rate of teenage pregnancy. Here they talk openly about their views.

Whilst Claire (16) raved about an after-school session for teenagers at her local family planning clinic, she could spot numerous flaws. 'Clinics are so badly publicised. I walked past one near me loads of times because it's just a little shop with blinds in the windows. It's trying to discourage teenage pregnancies but it's only open on a Thursday night and it rations the number of condoms it gives out.'

Teenagers agree that once they are sexually active, they need a sustainable, friendly source of contraception, advice and support. Yet cost is a significant barrier. 'It might be an idea to have free condoms in sixth-form common rooms or on racks at the door of the chemist,' said Bronwen, 13. 'That way, you can pick them up as you walk out.'

Many liked the immediacy of school as a place where contraceptives could be distributed more readily, but they had reservations. Bronwen worried that if condom machines were placed in toilets 'there would be too much stigma attached to using them'.

'A health visitor or visiting doctor to speak to young people about sexual health generally and provide contraception would work.' 'My school nurse is the last person on earth I'd go to with a headache, let alone a suspected pregnancy or for contraception,' admitted Jo, 18. Though teenagers see contraceptives as the key to preventing pregnancy, knowledge is patchy. 'We don't know a lot about the coil and other IUDs but we know a lot about condoms and the Pill,' said Alice, 15.

Abdul believed doing more to encourage safe sex is, 'Not about promoting contraception to young people, but about education.' 15-year-old Tom concluded, 'People should know there are other measures such as the "morning-after" pill. (This is now called Emergency Contraception.) The government should take action and have an advertising campaign to spread the word.'

> *'People should know there are other measures such as the "morning-after" pill. The government should take action and have an advertising campaign to spread the word.'*

Cutting teenage pregnancy: children's recommendations
- Deliver sex education through open lessons, where teenagers and children as young as five choose topics.
- Give young people access to a range of educators – teachers, parents, professionals (trained outsiders you'll never see again!), educational drama groups, peers.
- Discuss abuse and consent in sex education classes.
- Raise the consequences of becoming pregnant – don't stop at how to use contraceptives.
- Address gender issues in relation to sex and promote assertiveness.

■ This article was produced by Rachel Bulford, Daniel Blackwood and Darrell Philip, 18, Oliver Robertson, 17, Karen Loughrey, Anna Chandwani, Steven Boyle, Lindsay Marchant, Amy Wood, all 16, Ruth Sewell, 15, and Kierra Box, 14. All names have been changed The article is from X-press the IPPF newsletter for and by young people.

© International Planned Parenthood Federation (IPPF)

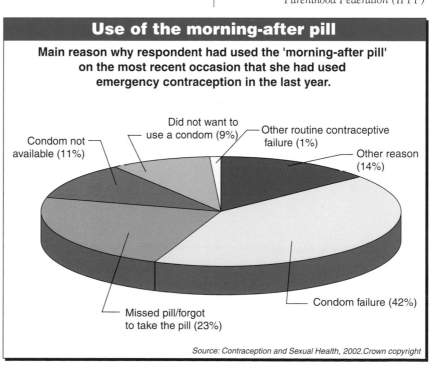

### Use of the morning-after pill

**Main reason why respondent had used the 'morning-after pill' on the most recent occasion that she had used emergency contraception in the last year.**

- Did not want to use a condom (9%)
- Other routine contraceptive failure (1%)
- Other reason (14%)
- Condom not available (11%)
- Other reason (14%)
- Condom failure (42%)
- Missed pill/forgot to take the pill (23%)

*Source: Contraception and Sexual Health, 2002. Crown copyright*

# The teenage girls whose 'career' choice is pregnancy

Young girls who dislike school are more likely to become teenage mothers, according to a study.

They may see pregnancy as preferable to staying at school or starting a career.

Research suggests that youngsters who do not like school are more likely to have sex before 16 and to expect to become parents before the age of 20 than those who enjoy being at school.

Yet the study found no difference between sexual knowledge among the two groups of teenagers.

Family campaigners said last night that the research disproves the contention that lack of sex education is a major cause of teenage pregnancy.

Robert Whelan, director of Family and Youth Concern, said: 'The Government's strategy to prevent teenage sex by providing sex education at ever younger ages and handing out condoms and other contraceptives is doomed to failure.

### By Jenny Hope, Medical Correspondent

'It should be scrapped and started again from scratch because this study shows for some girls getting pregnant can be a lifestyle choice.'

Researchers surveyed more than 8,000 pupils aged 13 and 14 from central and southern England about sexual knowledge, attitudes and behaviour.

> **Some young girls who believed they had no chance of a job or getting married might consider pregnancy a better option**

They found that dislike of school was linked to a greater risk of teenage pregnancy, according to the study – published yesterday in the *Journal of Epidemiology and Community Health*.

Compared to students who enjoyed school, those who did not like school were more likely to have had sex by 16 and expect to be parents by 20.

The study was carried out by the Social Science Research Unit, based at the Institute of Education, London University.

Researcher Vicki Strange said: 'Young people who dislike school might be more likely to see teenage pregnancy as inevitable or as a positive alternative to continuing education or a career.'

She said around one in five youngsters said they disliked school. But the study did not analyse truancy rates, which have been previously linked with teenage pregnancy.

She added: 'It may be it's something considered by young people if they don't think further education is for them, and it's the first time young people have been asked about their attitudes to school.

'But it's a hypothesis, not a hard conclusion, as we did not ask them if they intended to get pregnant.

'However, this possibility if confirmed in future studies would have important implications for teachers and educational and social policymakers.'

The UK has one of the highest teenage pregnancy rates in the developed world, with 31 births per 1,000 girls aged between 15 and 19 in 1998 although the rate has been falling.

The number of girls having underage sex has also doubled in the last ten years, according to official reports.

Mr Whelan said some young girls who believed they had no chance of a job or getting married might consider pregnancy a better option.

'They will qualify for accommodation and income support for 16 years and in the circumstances it might even seem a rational choice to some people.

'But being a single mum is not an easy option and we should be saying clearly that it limits your life chances.

'The sex education approach championed by the Government does not address the real issues.'

Mr Whelan added: 'For (Labour MP) Diane Abbott, it is relatively simple to spend £10,000 to ensure her son does not go to a local school in Hackney but what about all those children who have no choice?

'It is up to the Government to rethink its priorities.'

© The Daily Mail
October 2003

# Contraception and sexual health

In 2001/02 the most common forms of contraception used by women aged under 50 were the contraceptive pill (used by 28 per cent of women), the male condom (used by 21 per cent of women), and sterilisation (10 per cent of women had been sterilised and 12 per cent had a partner who had had a vasectomy), according to a report published today by the Office for National Statistics.

A quarter (25 per cent) of women were not using any method of contraception, and half of these women (13 per cent of all women aged 16-49) were not currently in a heterosexual relationship.

## Contraceptive use among women aged under 50

The use of the contraceptive pill and male condom were associated with age:

- Women aged under 30 were more likely to use the contraceptive pill than older women.
- The use of both the contraceptive pill and the male condom fell as respondents' age increased.
- Women aged 18-34 were more likely to be using the contraceptive pill than the male condom. Among women aged 40 and over this pattern is reversed.
- The likelihood of a woman having been sterilised or having a partner who had had a vasectomy rose with age.

## Women 'at risk' of pregnancy

Three-fifths (60 per cent) of women aged 16-49 were 'at risk' of pregnancy (that is, they were in a heterosexual relationship but were neither pregnant nor protected by their own or their partner's sterilisation). Eighty-eight per cent of women 'at risk' of pregnancy were currently using a method of contraception. Eight per cent were not using any method of contraception because of infertility, the menopause or they wanted to become pregnant, and a further four per cent were not using contraception for other reasons.

Almost half (47 per cent) of women 'at risk' of pregnancy were currently using the contraceptive pill.

## Emergency contraception

Over nine in ten (94 per cent) women aged 16-49 had heard of hormonal emergency contraception (the 'morning-after pill') and 46 per cent had heard of the emergency inter-uterine device (IUD).

Half (49 per cent) of women who had heard of the 'morning-after pill' knew that it remains effective up to 72 hours after intercourse. Only 12 per cent of women who had heard of the emergency IUD knew that it remains effective up to 5 days after intercourse.

Seven per cent of women aged 16-49 had used the 'morning-after pill' at least once during the year prior to interview. Women aged under 20 were twice as likely as those aged 20 and over to have used the 'morning-after pill' at least once in the past year (for example, 21 per cent aged 18-19 compared with 9 per cent aged 25-29).

The most popular source used by women to obtain the 'morning-after pill' was their own GP or practice nurse (43 per cent). A third (31 per cent) had obtained the 'morning-after pill' from a family planning clinic and 20 per cent from a chemist or pharmacy.

Between 2000/01 and 2001/02 there was a fall in the proportion of women who had obtained the 'morning-after pill' from their own

GP or practice nurse (59 per cent compared with 43 per cent): this may largely be explained by the ability, from January 2001, to obtain the 'morning-after pill' from a chemist or pharmacy.

### Family planning services

Three in five (60 per cent) women aged 16-49 had received family planning advice in the five years prior to interview. The majority of these women had visited their own GP or practice nurse (79 per cent) for this purpose and slightly more than a third (36 per cent) had visited a family planning clinic.

### Sterilisation and vasectomies

Ten per cent of women aged 16-49 and 15 per cent of men aged 16-69 had had an operation to make them sterile.

Among women the likelihood of having had an operation to become sterile rose with age.

Over nine in ten (92 per cent) women who had been sterilised had had their operation carried out by the NHS compared with only two-thirds (66 per cent) of men.

### Sexual behaviour

Thirteen per cent of men aged 16-69 and nine per cent of women aged 16-49 had had more than one sexual partner in the year prior to interview. Men and women aged under 25 were those most likely to have had multiple sexual partners.

### Condom use

Two-fifths (41 per cent) of men aged 16-69 and just under half (48 per

---

*Television programmes remained the main source of information about HIV/AIDS and other sexually transmitted infections*

---

cent) of women aged 16-49 who had had a sexual relationship in the last year said that they had used a male condom in the year prior to interview. When men and women of the same age are compared there is little difference between the sexes in their use of the male condom.

The only statistically significant differences between men and women were found among those in their twenties: in this age group men were more likely than women to have used a male condom in the year prior to interview (for example, 83 per cent of men aged 20-24 compared with 66 per cent of women in the same age group).

Respondents were most likely to have used a male condom in the last year if they were young (the proportion of men and women who had used a condom in the last year fell as age increased) or had multiple sexual partners in the last year.

### Knowledge of sexually transmitted infections

Respondents were asked whether they felt that their behaviour had been influenced by their knowledge of HIV/AIDS and other sexually transmitted infections:

- Over three-fifths of men and women said that their behaviour had not been affected (65 per cent of men aged 16-69 and 62 per cent of women aged 16-49).
- Three in ten men aged 16-69 and women aged 16-49 said that they use a condom more often than they used to (29 per cent and 30 per cent respectively).
- Six per cent of men aged 16-69 and seven per cent of women aged 16-49 said that they have fewer one-night stands.

Television programmes remained the main source of information about HIV/AIDS and other sexually transmitted infections (40 per cent).

Since 2000/01 the proportion of men aged 16-69 and women aged 16-49 who correctly identified Chlamydia as a sexually transmitted infection increased from 35 per cent to 45 per cent of men and among women rose from 65 per cent to 73 per cent.

Notes

1. The Omnibus Survey is a multi-purpose survey carried out by the ONS each month on behalf of a range of government departments and other public and non-profit making bodies.
2. Details of the policy governing the release of new data are available from the press office.
3. National Statistics are produced to high professional standards set out in the National Statistics Code of Practice. They undergo regular quality assurance reviews to ensure that they meet customer needs. They are produced free from any political interference.

■ This report presents the results of a survey for the Department of Health on contraception and sexual health carried out in 2001/02 as part of the National Statistics Omnibus Survey. Reports were also published with the results of four earlier surveys conducted in 1997/98, 1998/99, 1999/2000 and 2000/01. This report includes an examination of any significant changes in the data between 2000/01 and 2001/02.

*© Crown copyright 2003*

# The teenage sex epidemic

**Sexual diseases out of control. Morning-after pills doled out in schools. Condoms given away with magazines. Classroom videos encouraging oral sex. It is any wonder that our sex-obsessed teenagers have the highest rate of pregnancy in Europe?**

The girl is 14 years old and, while she is not yet proficient in all her lessons at school, there is one subject on which she is an expert – sex. All her friends talk about it. In class, she watches a Government-backed video – made especially for children of her age – in which she is encouraged to experiment with sexual positions and to consider oral sex if she's nervous of 'going all the way'.

In her lunch hour, she picks up a copy of her favourite magazine, *Sugar*, which is running a 'free condom for every reader' promotion (the magazine's target readership is 12 to 17). Back home, she settles down in front of her computer and logs on to 'likeitis', the sex web site for children set up by the charity Marie Stopes International. In the section headed 'first time for girls', she is reassured that 'sex won't be perfect the first time but make sure your contraception is sorted so you won't worry about getting pregnant'.

If the girl is left in any doubt as to what sex is all about, she can always consult her handy 'Good Grope Guide', part of the *Schools Sex Manual* published by the Brook Association. Mind you, she's probably a bit too old for it, since it's directed at 13-year-olds.

Armed with all this explicit information, she is now ready to have sex – and she certainly needn't worry about getting pregnant.

If she can't persuade her partner to use the condom supplied by *Sugar*, she can simply pop in to see the school nurse at break time for a morning-after pill.

If by chance she does fall pregnant, it won't be the end of the world. She's seen the Family Planning Association booklet aimed at 14- to 16-year-olds which reassures her that abortion is 'nothing to worry about'. No problem, then.

---

*By Natalie Clarke*

---

With influences like these, is it any wonder the result is the sexualisation of our nation's children and, with it, the making of a potential tragedy.

Britain is the teenage pregnancy capital of Europe; abortion is at an all-time high and we are in the grip of a huge epidemic of sexually transmitted infections which is threatening the fertility of the next generation.

## Britain is the teenage pregnancy capital of Europe; abortion is at an all-time high

Dr Kevin Fenton, of the Government's Health Protection Agency, says: 'We are facing a sex timebomb and there is growing concern that the health and fertility of an entire generation is at risk. It is a public health crisis.'

The statistics make disturbing reading. The number of teenagers using the morning-after pill has more than doubled since it became available over-the-counter in 2001.

According to figures from the Contraception and Sexual Health survey, carried out by the Office for National Statistics earlier this year, one in five 16-year-old girls takes the emergency contraception each year, and some use it repeatedly.

There have been reports of schools and clinics offering the morning-after pill – it was, of course, the Government's initiative to make it available in schools – to girls as young as 11. The Government has also given its approval for contraceptives to be handed out at school.

Government figures show that one in four girls has sex before the age of 16, while a recent survey by the Institute of Education and University College London showed that one youngster in every 14 has sex by the time they are 13 – and that, hardly surprisingly, many deeply regret it.

Among girls, 36 per cent were 'unhappy' over losing their virginity

### Source of information about STIs

**Source of information respondent learnt most about HIV/AIDS and other sexually transmitted infections by sex and age**

| Men aged 16-69 and women aged 16-49 | | | | Great Britain: 2002/03 | |
|---|---|---|---|---|---|
| Main source of information about HIV/AIDS and other STIs | Sex | | | Age | |
| | Men | Women | 16-24 | 25-59 | 50+ |
| TV programmes | 35% | 35% | 22% | 37% | 40% |
| TV advertisements | 26% | 19% | 20% | 24% | 22% |
| Newspapers, magazines, books | 22% | 23% | 15% | 22% | 29% |
| Government information leaflet | 2% | 3% | 1% | 3% | 2% |
| Friends or family | 2% | 3% | 4% | 3% | 1% |
| GP | 1% | 2% | 2% | 2% | 0% |
| Family planning clinic | 0% | 2% | 1% | 1% | - |
| GUM or sexual health clinic in hospital | 0% | 1% | 1% | 1% | - |
| Internet** | 6% | 7% | 28% | 2% | 0 |
| Somewhere else | 5% | 5% | 5% | 5% | 5% |
| **Total** | **100%** | **100%** | **100%** | **100%** | **100%** |
| Base | 2914 | 2193 | 873 | 3192 | 1043 |

*Source: Contraception and Sexual Health, 2002.Crown copyright*

at 13, and 18 per cent said 'it should never have happened'. Even among boys, some 32 per cent admitted they regretted having early sex.

The Government takes the politically correct, but highly contentious view that sex among youngsters is simply a lifestyle choice, a hobby even.

Among those who support that view is the organisation Marie Stopes International, which argues that young people need easy access to contraceptives so they are familiar with them by the time they think about having sex.

But the increase in sexually transmitted diseases such as chlamydia and gonorrhoea suggests advice about safe sex is not being heeded. In the past seven years, diagnoses of these two diseases have more than doubled.

Of the 71,125 cases of chlamydia reported in 2001, 36 per cent were among young women under 20. A survey carried out by NOP for the Family Planning Association, suggests that, among under-16s, the infection rate is one in seven.

Sexual health experts fear the chlamydia epidemic in particular is a 'ticking timebomb' and that in ten to 15 years' time huge swathes of the female population could find they are infertile as a result.

Staff at some health clinics have warned the Government they can't cope with the demand for treatment from patients – some as young as 12. One south London specialist, Dr Mark Pakianathan, said around 40,000 people attended his clinic last year, double the number five years ago.

Yet anyone who dares to point out that having sex under the age of 16 is behaving illegally is vilified for standing in the way of the individual's right to choose.

Dr Fenton says: 'Maybe in our society we feel a bit reticent about pushing abstention, but it is girls we are worried about – because we do see higher rates of sexually transmitted infections (STIs) in girls than in boys.

'They start to have sex earlier and have partners who are much older. These older men tend to have multiple partners. A 16-year-old girl thinks she is in love with a 20-year-old guy, but he may have several girls on the go at the same time. Young people are also having unsafe sex because they are drunk at the time.'

Teenage girls seem to be getting increasingly predatory in their sexual behaviour, aping the mannerisms of boys. Binge drinking has become not just socially acceptable, but almost expected. Girls brag about one-night stands and those who do not join in endure taunts that they are old-fashioned.

Fourteen-year-old Shakara Rose, who lives with her mother, a nurse, in East London, says: 'It feels as though everyone's talking about sex – comparing notes and telling stories. Most girls want to impress the boys and there's lots of drinking and drug use, even at our age.'

Yet while Britain descends deeper into libertarianism, the situation in the US could not be more different, where a powerful new movement is sweeping the country preaching the virtues of abstinence. Teenage girls and boys attend conventions such as the Silver Ring Thing, in which they take a sacred vow to remain virgins until their wedding day.

A similar campaign, True Love Waits, was made famous when teenage pop icon Britney Spears signed up. To date, more than a million young Americans have signed covenant cards pledging to abstain from sex until they marry.

Teenagers across the country are being taught that not only is abstinence the morally and spiritually correct path to take, but that it is also the only certain method of preventing sexually transmitted diseases and pregnancy. So there is no pressure on them to grow up before

---

*'It feels as though everyone's talking about sex – comparing notes and telling stories. Most girls want to impress the boys and there's lots of drinking and drug use, even at our age'*

---

they are ready; they are able, say campaign organisers, to enjoy their childhood.

Such programmes are a priority of the Bush administration, which has recently ploughed funds to the tune of $117 million into them.

In the US, where abstinence education became widespread during the 1990s, the teenage pregnancy rate dropped by 20 per cent. Many commentators think this is the way forward in the UK, too.

Robert Whelan, of the Family Education Trust, says: 'The spread of sexual infection is appalling, but the fact is that still no one is prepared to tell children to abstain from having sex.'

The authorities in this country take a totally different approach. Their solution to under-age sex is to teach children about sex as early as possible. The Government is now advising that children aged nine be given sex education and be taught about such topics as puberty, reproduction, contraception and STIs.

The Liberal Democrats are going even further, proposing at their conference last month that children as young as seven learn about transsexuals and STIs.

As Robert Whelan explains: 'The argument is that it is better to teach them before they become sexually active. But it puts it into their minds when it wouldn't usually be there.

'Most nine- and ten-year-olds haven't got any idea about sex. Many of them find these lessons distressing, or it normalises the idea of being sexually active at such a young age.'

Such strategies are supported by a barrage of literature. One company called Healthwise produces a schools' sex education pack, *Taking Sex Seriously*, which includes information on bondage and wife-swapping together with a lesson on 'the full range of sexual activities'.

Though it is out of print, it is still recommended by local education authorities,.

James Kay, head of Healthwise, typifies today's attitude to teenage sex in his defence of the pack. 'Our approach is to promote empowerment of children,' he says.

Dr Colin Wilson, a psychiatrist and sex expert, believes these attitudes are deeply worrying. 'If you look at this trend within the social context, this is a natural continuation of the sexual revolution and the emancipation of women. But that doesn't mean we can't do anything to stop it – and we should stop it.

'It's physically bad, particularly for the girls, who end up with pelvic inflammatory disease and can be rendered sterile, and then there's the issue of teenage pregnancy.

'Plus they are not emotionally equipped at that age to deal with being dumped by these young boys who don't want an intense commitment.

'Many of these children are from broken homes and are craving stability, but sexual relationships at such a young age will make them even more confused. They will go on to have multiple sexual partners and have all the physical problems that go with that, as well as becoming disillusioned. They are more likely to drop out of school and get into drugs.

'We need to give education on the basic facts of life and the consequences, not teaching children how to have oral sex and handing out condoms.'

Dr Wilson says it is up to parents to teach their children a responsible attitude towards sex. 'They should be teaching their kids that nothing good comes out of under-age sex,' he says.

Sadly, however, many children do come from broken homes. The number of single-parent families has doubled to 1.75 million in 15 years. More than one child in four lives in a lone-parent household.

While it may be politically incorrect to say so, all the evidence suggests there is a direct correlation between children raised in one-parent families and a child's sexual behaviour.

Dr David Cowell, a consultant psychologist specialising in teenage behaviour, says: 'Young people who have secure family relationships are less likely to go on to have precocious or unsuitable relationships.

'Children who are lonely or don't have good relations with their family are desperate to have an intimate relationship because they feel their life has nothing in it. That's when things can go horribly wrong.

'I think there can be a problem with single-parent families. There is often difficulty about knowing where the boundaries are.

'Girls who grow up with good fathers, uncles and brothers are much more realistic about boys. Girls who go excessively over the top with boyfriends tend not to have grown up with men in a family environment, and see them as mysterious, exciting figures.'

So what is to be don? Many advocate a complete turnaround in attitudes and the introduction of abstinence education, as is being practised in the US.

Robert Whelan, of the Family Education Trust, says: 'The Government should be telling young people not to have sex yet, rather than telling them that sex is fine but they need to be using contraception.'

© The Daily Mail, October 2003

## In their own words . . . what the teenagers think

*Shakara Rose, 14, lives with her mother, a nurse, and elder brother and sister, in East London. Her father left home when she was two. She says:*
'There's so much stress at this age with schoolwork, and sex is just another big pressure. It's talked about really openly. So many girls have sex very young for the wrong reasons. They say : "I love him"; "I was drunk"; "I didn't want him to go off me". And there's lots of drinking and drug use, even at our age.

I haven't had sex yet, though I do feel a lot of pressure to, but it's not the right time for me. I know so many girls who've had sex really young and then had regrets about it later. While it's completely normal for 13- and 14-year-olds to have sex, that's not what I want for myself. In my year at least one or two in every ten has had sex. And in the year above, it's 90 per cent, which is virtually everyone except the Muslims and other kids from religious backgrounds.'

*Luke Elford, 17, lives with his mother, a gardener, and father, a computer consultant, in East London. He hopes to go to Cambridge University and become a barrister. He says:*
'I had sex at 13 and was much too young. I was still very childlike and more interested in football and computer games than girls. I'd gone away with my football team and during the trip a 16-year-old girl started to take an interest in me. She was touching me and giggling, but I didn't notice until it was spelt out to me. I'd never even kissed a girl before and I was shaking like a leaf.

I remember thinking it felt very strange and maybe I shouldn't be doing it, but there was so much adrenaline my feelings were suppressed.

When it was over, I didn't feel I could talk to anyone about it because I thought people would think I was lying. I wish I'd been older. I would have felt more able to say "No" when it didn't feel right.'

*Scarlet Winter, 17, lives with her mother, a local government officer, and stepfather, a project manager, in Bow, East London. She says:*
'The pressure on young people to grow up too fast is overwhelming. TV, magazines and the music industry don't seem to take respons-ibility for the influence they have.

After-school soaps such as *Hollyoaks* deal with issues including pregnancy and abortion, but it also leaves the 14- and 15-year-old viewer with the impression that sex at that age is what's expected. I'm pleased I waited until I was 17 and in a good relationship with a boy I love who loves me, too. He was a close friend before we started going out, so we knew and trusted each other. It was a huge relief to have got losing my virginity over and done with, though. There's so much focus on sex that you almost feel the odd one out to be a virgin.'

# Explicit sex lessons fail to cut teen pregnancies

**By Celia Hall,
Medical Editor**

Sex education programmes have failed to reduce teenage pregnancies, according to two new research studies.

A series of explicit sex education programmes in Scottish schools was found to be no better in cutting teenage pregnancies or risky sexual behaviour than standard sex education lessons.

The second study in the *British Medical Journal*, from Canada, which looked at 26 trials among pupils aged 11 to 18, found that pregnancy prevention programmes did not delay sexual intercourse, improve birth control or cut unwanted pregnancies.

Among the Canadian trials, four abstinence programmes and one sex-based school programme increased the pregnancies in girlfriends of boys taking part.

Researchers now believe that cultural influences are stronger than the influence of education even when teachers are specially trained and the courses carefully planned.

The Scottish study was led by Dr Daniel Wright, of Medical Research Council's social and public health sciences unit at Glasgow University.

The 8,430 youngsters aged 13 to 15 who took part in the specially designed Scottish programme about sex, called Share, were better informed and less likely to regret their sexual encounters.

Otherwise there were no significant differences. Two years later when nearly 6,000 of them were followed up, four per cent of the young women in the Share programme had become pregnant compared with 3.8 per cent in the control group.

> **'There had been some concern that the more open and frank lessons might encourage young people to experiment but we found no differences'**

When asked about recent sexual activity, 33.6 per cent of boys and 44.9 per cent of girls had sex without a condom compared with 34.9 per cent of boys and 44 per cent of girls in the control group.

About a third of the teenagers had sex for the first time in the year either after sessions with Share or with conventional sex education.

Researchers concluded that sex education alone was not enough to change behaviour.

Share, which stands both for Sexual Health and Relationships and Safe, Happy and Responsible, gave teachers five days of training and pupils aged 13 to 14 a programme of 10 sessions followed by 10 sessions in the next school year.

'There had been some concern that the more open and frank lessons might encourage young people to experiment but we found no differences,' said Marion Henderson, one of the researchers.

'We think the young people who experienced Share were better armed for their sexual lives but school is only one forum.'

Researchers now believe the whole-class approach may not work well as young people's needs differ. 'One idea is for drop-in centres at schools where young people could talk about concerns including sexual relationships,' Miss Henderson said.

Britain's teenage pregnancy rates are the highest in western Europe and, in England, the Department of Health is committed to halving by 2010 the rates in girls up to 18.

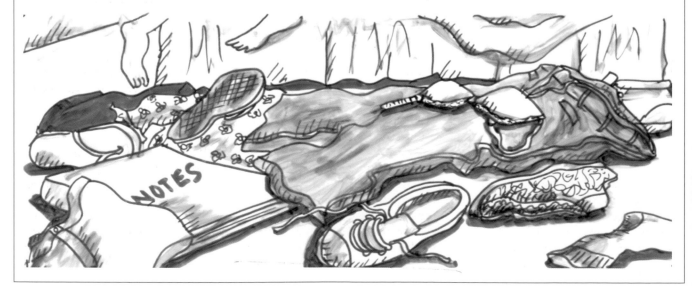

# Sex education that works

**By Simon Forrest, Director, Sex Education Forum, UK & Annabel Kanabus, Director, AVERT, UK**

## What is sex education?

Sex education, which is sometimes called sexuality education or sex and relationships education, is the process of acquiring information and forming attitudes and beliefs about sex, sexual identity, relationships and intimacy. It is also about developing young people's skills so that they make informed choices about their behaviour, and feel confident and competent about acting on these choices. It is widely accepted that young people have a right to sex education, partly because it is a means by which they are helped to protect themselves against abuse, exploitation, unintended pregnancies, sexually transmitted diseases and HIV/AIDS.[1, 2, 3, 4, 5]

## What are the aims of sex education?

Sex education seeks both to reduce the risks of potentially negative outcomes from sexual behaviour like unwanted or unplanned pregnancies and infection with sexually transmitted diseases, and to enhance the quality of relationships. It is also about developing young people's ability to make decisions over their entire lifetime. Sex education that works, by which we mean that it is effective, is sex education that contributes to this overall aim.

---

*Sex education seeks to reduce the risks of potentially negative outcomes from sexual behaviour*

---

## Forming attitudes and beliefs

Young people can be exposed to a wide range of attitudes and beliefs in relation to sex and sexuality. These sometimes appear contradictory and confusing. For example, some health

messages emphasis the risks and dangers associated with sexual activity and some media coverage promotes the idea that being sexually active makes a person more attractive and mature. Because sex and sexuality are sensitive subjects, young people and sex educators can have strong views on what attitudes people should hold, and what moral framework should govern people's behaviour – these too can sometimes seem to be at odds. Young people are very interested in the moral and cultural frameworks that bind sex and sexuality. They often welcome opportunities to talk about issues where people have strong views, like abortion, sex before marriage, lesbian and gay issues, and contraception and birth control. It is important to remember that talking in a balanced way about differences in opinion does not promote one set of views over another, or mean that one agrees with a particular view. Part of exploring and understanding cultural, religious and moral views is finding out that you can agree to disagree.

People providing sex education have attitudes and beliefs of their own about sex and sexuality and it is important not to let these influence negatively the sex education that they provide. For example, even if a person believes that young people should not have sex until they are married, this does not imply withholding important information about safer sex and contraception. Attempts to impose narrow moralistic views about sex and sexuality on young people through sex education have failed.[6] Rather than trying to deter or frighten young people away from having sex, effective sex education includes work on attitudes and beliefs, coupled with skills development, that enables young people to choose whether or not to have a sexual relationship taking into account the potential risks of any sexual activity.

Effective sex education also provides young people with an opportunity to explore the reasons why people have sex, and to think about how it involves emotions, respect for oneself and other people and their feelings, decisions and bodies. Young people should have the chance to explore gender differences and how ethnicity and sexuality can influence people's feelings and options.[7] They should be able to decide for themselves what the positive qualities of relationships are. It is important that they understand how bullying, stereotyping, abuse and exploitation can negatively influence relationships.

---

*Providing information through sex education is about finding out what young people already know and adding to their existing knowledge*

---

## So what information should be given to young people?

Young people get information about sex and sexuality from a wide range of sources including each other, through the media including advertising, television and magazines, as well as leaflets, books and websites (such as www.avert.org) which are intended to be sources of information about sex and sexuality. Some of this will be accurate and some inaccurate. Providing information through sex education is therefore about finding out what young people already know and adding to their existing knowledge and correcting any misinformation they may have. For example, young people may have heard that condoms are not effective against HIV/AIDS or that there is a cure for AIDS. It is important to provide information which corrects mistaken beliefs. Without correct information young people can put themselves at greater risk.

Information is also important as the basis on which young people can developed well-informed attitudes and views about sex and sexuality. Young people need to have information on all the following topics:
- Sexual development;
- Reproduction;
- Contraception;
- Relationships.

They need to have information about the physical and emotional changes associated with puberty and sexual reproduction, including fertilisation and conception, and about sexually transmitted diseases, including HIV/AIDS. They also need to know about contraception and birth control including what contraceptives there are, how they work, how people use them, how they decide what to use or not, and how they can be obtained. In terms of information about relationships they need to know about what kinds of relationships there are, about love and commitment, marriage and partnership, and the law relating to sexual behaviour and relationships as well as the range of religious and cultural views on sex and sexuality and sexual diversity. In addition, young people should be provided with information about abortion, sexuality, and confidentiality, as well as about the range of sources of advice and support that is available in the community and nationally.

*References*
1 United Nations Universal Declaration of Human Rights http://www.un.org/rights/HRToday/ (accessed 15.04.02)
2 European Convention on the Exercise of Children's Rights www.eurochild.gla.ac.uk/documents/coe/Treaties/ETS No 160.htm
3 United Nations Declaration on the Rights of the Child, www.un.org/rights/HRToday/ (accessed 15.04.02)
4 United Nations General Assembly, Declaration of commitment on HIV/AIDS 2nd August 2001 www.un.org/ga/aids/docs/aress262.pdf (accessed 15.04.02)
5 International Planned Parenthood Foundation www.ippf.org/charter/summary.htm (accessed 15.04.02)
6 National Campaign to Prevent Teenage Pregnancy (1998) *Evaluating abstinence-only interventions.*
7 Meyrick, J. and Swann, C. (1998) *Reducing the rate of teenage conceptions: an overview of effectiveness of interventions and programmes aimed at reducing unintended conceptions in young people.* London: Health Education Authority

■ The above information is from AVERT's web site which can be found at www.avert.org

# Cut benefits for mothers in teens, says family group

## By Sarah Womack, Social Affairs Correspondent

Teenage mothers should have their benefits reduced and made conditional on them living with their parents, family campaigners say today.

The Family Education Trust said Britain needed to learn from Holland where unmarried teenage mothers were stigmatised and becoming a lone parent was likely to have economic and social costs.

Robert Whelan, the charity's director, said conventional wisdom said Dutch teenage pregnancies were lower because of explicit and early sex education.

Britain has one of the world's highest teenage pregnancy rates and the highest in Europe. But research by the Dutch sociologist Joost van Loon, commissioned by the trust, found that sex education in the Netherlands did not start at a younger age, was not more explicit and did not conform to any single 'Dutch' model.

The influences of the churches was stronger, however, and the trust believed the restricted income support system for teenage parents in the Netherlands could be a major factor in deterring girls from having children.

Mr Whelan said young Britons were 'encouraged to regard sexual relations from an early age as unobjectionable and desirable as long as they use contraception'.

'We need to learn the lessons of the Netherlands. Benefits to teenage mothers should be reduced and made conditional on living with their parents or in supervised hostel accommodation. Public policy should also be reviewed to see if there are ways in which the traditional family, based on marriage, could be shored up rather than undermined.'

Birth rates are seven times higher in England and Wales for the 15-19 age group than in Holland. Conception rates are four times higher.

Mr Whelan said stigma was 'one of the most powerful means of controlling behaviour considered destructive to society'. The Government was failing to bolster family life despite knowing that sexual activity was higher when girls grew up without fathers.

The trust is linked to the pressure group Family and Youth Concern which opposes groups such as Brook and the Sex Education Forum which promote comprehensive sex advice and easier availability of contraceptives for young teenagers.

# 'Tackle boys to tackle teen pregnancies'

*The Government needs to target hard-to-reach groups such as boys, young men and ethnic minorities to make an impact on teenage pregnancy, says a health advisory group.*

In its second annual report, the Independent Advisory Group on Teenage Pregnancy said young people are becoming more confident about using sexual health services, but more needs to be done.

The group also made eight key recommendations to the Government on how to further tackle the difficult problem, including efforts to focus on young people from black and ethnic minority groups.

Chairwoman Lady Winifred Tumim said there had been encouraging progress to reduce the number of teenagers falling pregnant during the past year – but it was vital to keep the pressure up.

The latest figures revealed a 10 per cent cut in the rate of conceptions among under-18s, and an 11 per cent fall among under-16s since 1998.

The report's authors call for a national information campaign to be intensified to target specific groups of youngsters who are disadvantaged or hard to reach.

They said that boys and young men were 'half the solution' to reducing pregnancies and more needed to be done to get them involved in 'sex and relationship education' in school.

---

*Boys and young men are 'half the solution' to reducing pregnancies and more needed to be done to get them involved in 'sex and relationship education' in school*

---

The report also recommended that personal, social and health education is made part of the statutory curriculum, with a specialist teacher on the subject in all secondary schools by 2006.

They also push for a new advertising campaign to ensure that those under 16 know they have the same rights to confidentiality as adults when seeking advice from health professionals about contraception, sex and relationships.

Minister for Children Margaret Hodge said the report gave 'important, independent recognition' of the Government's commitment to tackling teenage pregnancy.

'Our Teenage Pregnancy Strategy, the first of its kind, is based on the best available research evidence which shows that the key to success is an approach which involves education, health, social services, the media, parents and young people themselves,' she said.

The advisory group, established in 2000, provides advice to the Government and monitors the success of the Teenage Pregnancy Strategy.

The strategy aims to halve the under-18 conception rate by 2010 and increase the number of teenage mothers in education, training and employment to 60 per cent.

© *The Daily Mail*
*July, 2003*

# Juniors' sex education 'should be compulsory'

By Sarah Womack, Social Affairs Correspondent

Sex education should be made compulsory in primary schools if Britain's high rate of teenage pregnancy is to be reduced, a group which advises ministers will recommend today.

The Independent Advisory Group on Teenage Pregnancy, which tracks the progress of the Government strategy, wants sex education for infants to be 'rooted' by law in lessons on relationships.

But the recommendation will upset religious groups and family campaigners who think the innocence of youngsters should be protected.

At present, many primary schools teach four- to seven-year-olds that 'humans can produce offspring'. Between seven and 11, pupils learn more about human reproduction and HIV.

However, the precise content and tone of such lessons is left to the discretion of schools because policies on sex education are set by school governors in consultation with parents.

Parents also have the right to withdraw their children from sex education lessons they feel inappropriate.

The advisory group says teachers lack confidence when it comes to teaching about sex.

It is 'disappointed' that sex education is not embraced by primary schools, 'particularly considering evidence of early pubertal changes', and recommends that sex education forms part of the statutory curriculum at all key stages. Key stage one starts at five.

Simon Blake, from the National Children's Bureau and former head of the Sex Education Forum, said: 'You have got to make sure young people understand about relationships and sex before they start puberty.'

The Department for Education said: 'Effective sex and relationship education does not encourage early sexual experimentation.'

However, ministers are split on the issue.

David Blunkett, the Home Secretary, believes infants should not be exposed on a compulsory basis to such teaching while Margaret Hodge, the children's minister, and Tessa Jowell, the former health minister, are thought to support a widening of sex education to youngsters.

Earlier this year two academics, one of whom was also a Church of England priest, said that by nine, children were picking up information about sex from a variety of sources and unless they were taught about it they would get much of their information from the media.

Robert Whelan, director of Family and Youth Concern, was scathing about the group's report.

'People have been saying "more sex education" for decades. There is no research in the world that suggests sex education in primary schools has any effect in reducing conceptions and sexually transmitted infections.

'This group has simply run out of ideas.' In 2001 there were 38,439 conceptions in England to under-18s. Around a third end in abortion.

The Government's aim is to halve the under-18 conception rate by 2010, and increase to 60 per cent the participation of mothers in education and employment.

But casting doubt on the accuracy of existing figures, the advisory group says that ministers need 'a more robust method' for collecting data on teenage pregnancies among those children who are looked after by social services.

It adds that special efforts must be made in dealing with teenage pregnancies among young people with learning disabilities.

© Telegraph Group Limited, London 2003

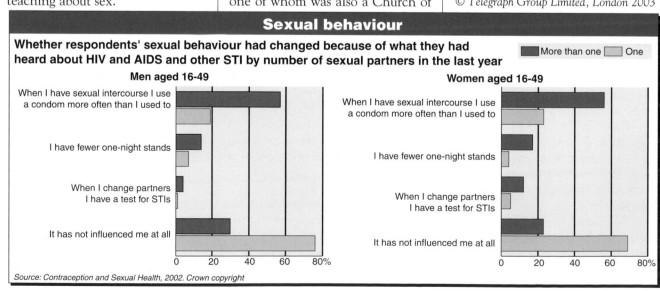

## Sexual behaviour

**Whether respondents' sexual behaviour had changed because of what they had heard about HIV and AIDS and other STI by number of sexual partners in the last year**

■ More than one ☐ One

**Men aged 16-49**

- When I have sexual intercourse I use a condom more often than I used to
- I have fewer one-night stands
- When I change partners I have a test for STIs
- It has not influenced me at all

0 20 40 60 80%

**Women aged 16-49**

- When I have sexual intercourse I use a condom more often than I used to
- I have fewer one-night stands
- When I change partners I have a test for STIs
- It has not influenced me at all

0 20 40 60 80%

Source: Contraception and Sexual Health, 2002. Crown copyright

# Teenage conception rates down

## Health Minister announces increase in funding for sustained action on Teenage Pregnancy Strategy

Figures published today by the Office of National Statistics show that teenage conception rates fell for the third year in a row. In 2001, conception rates in under-18s were 3% lower than in 2000. The total reduction since 1998 is 9% which means that around 8,000 pregnancies in girls under 18 have been prevented. Conception rates in under-16s in 2001 were 4.5% lower than in 2000, with an overall reduction of over 10% since 1998.

Public Health Minister Hazel Blears welcomed today's figures and responded by announcing an additional £40 million to support the implementation of the Government's Teenage Pregnancy Strategy over the next three years.

She said: 'These figures show very encouraging progress towards our goal of halving the under 18 conception rate by 2010. Our Teenage Pregnancy Strategy, the first of its kind, is based on the best available research evidence which shows that the key to success is an approach which involves education, health, social services, the media, parents and young people themselves.

'The 9% reduction over three years reflects an enormous amount of work and commitment at a local level towards helping young people make safe, informed choices and supporting teenage parents to improve the quality of life for them and their children. The increase in funding will enable local areas to build on the progress made so far. Tackling Britain's unacceptably high rates of teenage pregnancy remains a key priority.'

The main targets of the Teenage Pregnancy Strategy are to halve the rate of conceptions in under-18s by 2010, with an interim reduction of 15% by 2004; set a firmly established

downward trend in the under-16s conception rates by 2010 and to increase to 60% the participation of teenage parents in education and work to reduce their risk of long-term social exclusion.

Each top-tier local authority area has its own ten-year teenage preg-nancy strategy to reach locally agreed targets, led by a teenage pregnancy co-ordinator working with repre-sentatives from local Primary Care Trusts, social services, education, housing, Connexions and other relevant partners.

Initiatives undertaken in 2002 as part of the Government's Teenage Pregnancy Strategy include:

- A new professional development programme and certificate in Sex and Relationships Education for teachers as part of Personal, Social and Health Education in schools
- A campaign – Getting it Right for Teenagers in Your Practice – run with the Royal College of General Practitioners and Royal College of Nursing to improve young people's access to advice in primary care.
- A series of regional seminars for schools and Primary Care Trusts on school-based health services.
- Twenty Sure Start Plus pilots to co-ordinate a comprehensive support package for teenage parents, including tailored midwifery and health visiting support and help with returning to education, training and employment.
- New resources for young fathers to increase their involvement in the care of their children and improve support services from health professionals.
- Support for parents in talking to their children about sex and relationships with Parentline Plus through media work and a support Helpline.
- A new resource – *Diverse Communities: Identity and Teenage Pregnancy* – to support local areas to work inclusively with groups from a range of black and minority communities and faith groups.
- A national media campaign in teenage magazines and local radio, achieving over 70% recognition among 13- 17-year-olds and supported by a Helpline taking 1.4 million calls a year.
- A new evidence briefing published by the Health Development Agency this week which confirms the research evidence for the Teenage Pregnancy Strategy and guidance on the most effective ways of working.

# Is abstinence the answer?

**Many here believe little can be done to stop the sexual explosion among teenagers. But in America a new movement proves there IS another way**

A thousand teenagers are packed into a church hall in Knoxville, Tennessee. They are about to take a sacred vow that will shape the way they lead the rest of their lives. As the lights dim, each of them takes a silver ring from their pocket.

Their voices chime in unison as, with great solemnity, they place the ring on their finger and make their pledge: 'I agree to wear a silver ring as a sign of my pledge to abstain from sexual behaviour. On my wedding day, I will present my ring to my spouse signifying my faith and commitment.'

They have made their choice; they have stated, in public, their commitment to chastity and their rejection of the permissive values of the modern world. Their intention is to reclaim the moral code of restraint that was embraced by their grandparents before the sexual revolution changed everything.

They are doing so at the latest Silver Ring Thing (SRT) event, one of a growing number of phenomenally popular chastity movements sweeping across the US.

America gas suffered a sexual counter-revolution, which many believe is long overdue – and it's gathering momentum.

As in Britain, America has seen an epidemic of sexually transmitted infections (STIs) among the young, and a dispiritingly high teenage pregnancy rate. But now, the 'safe sex' message is being eclipsed by the growing belief in the virtues of abstinence.

Teenagers across the country are being taught that not only is abstinence the morally correct path to take, but that it is also the only certain method of preventing STIs and pregnancy.

Not only that, they are taught that sex before marriage is likely to have harmful physical and psychological effects. And as for having children outside marriage, that will lead to damaging consequences for the child, the child's parents and society.

This tough moral stance on teenage sex has become a priority of the Bush administration, which has ploughed $117 million into such programmes.

As well as abstinence education in schools, chastity organisations such as Silver Ring Thing – which received a $700,000 (£450,000) federal grant earlier this year – are finding followers in ordinary teenagers everywhere.

A similar campaign, True Love Waits, was made famous when teenage pop icon Britney Spears signed up. More than a million young Americans have signed covenant cards pledging to abstain from sex until they marry.

> *Teenagers are being taught that not only is abstinence the morally correct path to take, but that it is also the only certain method of preventing STIs and pregnancy*

Silver Ring Thing – the name was temporary, but stuck – was set up by Denny Pattyn, a father of three girls from Yuma, Arizona, in 1995. Pattyn was shocked to learn that Yuma had the highest number of teenage pregnancies in the state, and was determined to do something about it.

The organisation now has more than 15,000 members nationwide, most aged between 12 and 22. Every member wears a $12 (£8) silver ring – a thin band for girls, slightly thicker for boys – as a sign of their commitment to the abstinence pledge.

'This is what I call the "Cesspool Generation", the ones who are suffering the catastrophic effects of the sexual revolution', says Pattyn. 'Abstinence is the safest option, emotionally and physically. A teenager's body is a magnet for STIs.'

At a convention in Tennessee last month, more than 500 youngsters signed up for a silver ring before the show had begun. By the evening's end, 740 had taken the Silver Ring Thing Oath.

Among them was 15-year-old Chelsea Ellis and her best friend Kathryn Wilson, also 15. 'I want to wear the ring to show the world that I believe having sex before marriage is wrong,' says Chelsea.

'It just leads to so many complications. Five or six girls get pregnant at my school every year,' adds Kathryn. 'They're so stupid. I don't want to end up like them.'

The show is a lively mixture of music, comedy sketches and talks – entertainment with a serious message. Condoms, the audience is told, cannot protect body and mind; each time they have sex with a different partner they 'leave behind a piece of their heart'.

One of the organisers is 25-year-old Deb Ott, who is what is termed a 'start-over' – someone who started having sex at a young age, later regretted it and decided to abstain from sex until she was safely wed.

'Like many high school students, I was 16 when I lost my virginity,' says Deb, SRT's National Training Director, who is now married. 'There was a lot of peer pressure. I was the last virgin among my friends.

'My generation is paying the price of our parents' sexual liberation. They have set us a very bad example to follow.'

Not all the young students who attend SRT events are virgins. Those who have been sexually active are invited to attend and begin a 'Second Virginity' phase.

It's an approach which is already having an impact. In America, there has been a 20 per cent reduction in teenage pregnancies in the past ten years.

Compare the fresh-faced optimism of the teenage girls at the SRT Convention with teenage mother Julie Olive from Bolton, who, at 16, already regrets having been sexually precocious.

Her days now revolve around looking after her son, Michael, who has cerebral palsy and requires round-the-clock care. She is brutally frank about her situation. 'If I'd known sex could bring all this grief, I'd probably still be a virgin,' she says.

Of course, for Julie, who had her baby at 15, there is no going back. The pregnancy was the result of a nine-month relationship with a boy her age. 'He was nothing special, just a boyfriend,' she admits. 'I'd been out drinking with friends at the time and it just happened.'

This was despite the fact that she was on the pill at her mother's insistence. One might question the wisdom of such advice, as it clearly was seen by her as a licence to have under-age sex. Julie, in her naively, kept forgetting to take it.

She is painfully aware of all the things she is missing out on. 'I love Michael, but I regret having sex and getting pregnant so young. There's so much more I could have done with my life.'

It is a depressing assessment of her young life, yet stories similar to Julie's are now dispiritingly familiar across the country.

Britain appears to be in little danger of losing its unfortunate distinction of being the teenage pregnancy capital of Europe. In 2001, 40,966 girls under 18 became pregnancy. Of those, 5,610 were 15; 1,883 were 14; and 398 were under 14.

In an attempt to deal with the crisis, the Government has set up the Teenage Pregnancy Unit. As part of its work, the TPU has requested that every local authority produce a 'teenage pregnancy strategy'.

These strategies make perplexing reading. The general gist appears to be that girls have a 'right' to explore their sexuality without risk of pregnancy, and it is somehow the local authority's responsibility to ensure they are armed with contraceptives.

There is no mention of the moral responsibility of the individual. East Kent's vision, for example, is that 'children and young people . . . be aware of and enjoy their sexuality'. Swindon takes the view that 'young women have the right to freedom from unplanned pregnancy and a fulfilling sex life'.

Kingston and Richmond state that 'it is a young person's right to expect that . . . all unwanted teenage conceptions are prevented as much as possible, by different agencies working together'.

This year alone, £16 million is being invested in the implementation of such strategies.

But Robert Whelan, of the Family Education Trust, believes they are doomed to failure.

'Whether it is appropriate for local authorities to facilitate these sexual adventures is a matter of opinion, but some of the assurances which they are giving to young people verge on the irresponsible,' he says.

'It would be imprudent for teenagers to embark on a vigorous sex life under the impression that anyone can guarantee them a "right" to escape unplanned pregnancies and sexually transmitted infections.'

Yet, for many young girls, becoming a single mother is practically an aspiration. A recent survey by the Family Education Trust, for example, found that 45 per cent of girls who had become pregnant had either wanted to or didn't mind if they did.

One of the crucial factors as to whether a teenage girl becomes

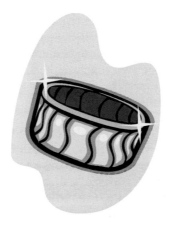

pregnant appears to be her social background. A girl from a broken home presided over by a struggling single mother may see the idea of a baby as a blessing that will give her a purpose in life.

Dr David Paton, an expert on teenage fertility at the University of Nottingham, agrees that all the evidence suggests that children from stable, two-parent families will wait until they're older before they have sex. 'Children brought up by two parents are far less likely to have sex under 16 – or even under 18,' he says. 'The main protective factor against underage sex and STIs is the two-parent family.'

Dr Paton says teenagers are getting mixed messages. 'On the one hand, sex under the age of 16 is illegal; on the other you are giving information which says, well, if you are going to do it, here's how to go about it.'

The irony is that abstinence, as has been proved in America, might actually make a difference. Its greatest supporters, indeed, could be teenagers themselves, relieved to be free of the tremendous pressure places on them to join the sexual merry-go-round.

A damning picture has emerged of a generation of young people who have become the unwitting victims of the great experiment in sexual liberality. They are children who are not allowed to be children, who are handed pills and condoms and placed under intolerable pressure to be sexually active, whether they are ready or not.

Not only is their fertility threatened by an epidemic of sexually transmitted infections, but many will end up becoming mothers when they are not yet out of their teems, often struggling alone because the fathers are inevitably too young and immature to take on the responsibility of raising a baby.

It is a devastating picture of modern society. So is there a new way forward? As we have seen in America, many young people want to embrace the traditional values that were swept aside in the wake of the sexual revolution. Perhaps the time has come to listen to them.

© *The Daily Mail*
*October 2003*

# Some facts and figures

## Lone parents

### A definition

It may seem unnecessary to define a 'lone' parent. For official purposes, however, a lone-parent family is one where: 'A mother or father living without a spouse (and not co-habiting) with his or her never-married dependent child or children aged either under 16 or from 16 to 19 and undertaking full-time education.'

This definition therefore includes people who are married but living on their own with the children of the family, and also those who are living with others who are not their partner (with parents for example).

### Some facts and figures

Analysis undertaken by the One Parent Families (OPF) shows the following:

*Becoming a lone parent*
- It is estimated that there are 1.75 million one-parent families in Britain today – this is nearly a quarter of all families;
- The number of one-parent families has trebled in the last 30 years, but the increase has recently slowed;
- Two in five marriages will ultimately end in divorce, but recent figures show the rate is at its lowest since 1984;
- The fastest growing group of lone parents is now single or never-married lone parents (however, this includes ex-cohabitees best described as separated).

*The children*
- More than one in five children is now cared for in a one-parent family – this equates to approximately 3 million children;
- In 2000, 142,000 children under 16 were affected by divorce, nearly twice as many as in 1971, but fewer than the highest figure of 176,000 in 1993;
- A third to a half of children will spend some time in a one-parent family;
- Approximately 25% of children were under five years old, and seven in ten were under ten years old.

*Demographics*
- Nine out of ten lone parents are women;
- Lone fathers are nearly three times as likely as lone mothers to be widowed and, like widows, they are likely to be older;
- The average age for a lone parent is 35;
- At any one time, less than 3% of all lone parents are teenagers.

### Challenging some myths
- Only 15% or one in seven lone mothers have never married or lived with their child's father;
- A one-parent family is now viewed as a 'stage' in family life that lasts on average about five and a half years;
- Never-married lone parents tend to be younger than other lone parents and are more likely to be on benefit. However, that group tends to have smaller families, take paid work and re-partner sooner;
- 35% of lone parents have experienced violence in their last relationship with three-quarters of them sustaining physical injuries.

Clearly, many families are now headed by a lone parent and millions of children live within such a family. However, the negative portrait of lone parenthood painted in the press and media is not necessarily accurate. Nevertheless, lone parents need specific types of support in order to ensure that they do not experience exclusion from employment and training opportunities. Support for this group is also key to the Government's pledge to cut child poverty.

■ The above information is an extract from *Moving Towards Inclusion – A Picture of Disadvantage in the South West* by the Skills and Learning Intelligence Module (SLIM).

© *The Skills and Learning Intelligence Module (SLIM)*

### Lone parents
#### Families with dependent children headed by lone parents[1]

| Great Britain | | | | Percentages | |
|---|---|---|---|---|---|
| | 1971 | 1981 | 1991 | 1999 | 2001[2] |
| **Lone mothers** | | | | | |
| Single | 1 | 2 | 6 | 8 | 9 |
| Widowed | 2 | 2 | 1 | 1 | 1 |
| Divorced | 2 | 4 | 6 | 6 | 6 |
| Separated | 2 | 2 | 4 | 4 | 4 |
| **All lone mothers** | 7 | 11 | 18 | 20 | 20 |
| | | | | | |
| Lone fathers | 1 | 2 | 1 | 2 | 2 |
| | | | | | |
| **All lone parents** | 8 | 13 | 19 | 22 | 22 |

1 Lone mothers (by their marital status) and lone fathers.
2 At Spring 2001

*Source: Social Trends 2002, Crown copyright*

# One child in four is being raised by a single parent

Nearly one in four children is being raised in a single-parent family, according to Census figures released in May 2003.

Another one in ten lives with step-parents or an unmarried couple.

The picture of family life at the outset of the 21st century emerged from the national headcount of the UK population taken two years ago last month.

The number of children living with lone parents – 2,672,000 – rose sharply over the previous decade and was double the figure recorded in the early 1980s.

Fewer than two-thirds of all youngsters now live with their two natural parents.

The continuing growth of single parenthood, fuelled by rising numbers of cohabiting parents who are statistically more likely to end their relationship after having children, means many youngsters are likely to face serious disadvantages at school and in later life.

Research has shown that the children of single parents are more likely to under-perform academically, to fall into crime or drug abuse in their teens and become single parents themselves.

More than 90 per cent of the single-parent families are headed by lone mothers, the Census showed.

Apart from children living with one parent, many more have seen their natural parents break up and now live with a stepfather or stepmother.

The statistics, which cover England and Wales, show some 725,000 children live in a stepfamily with married parents, while another 558,000 have a step-parent who lives with either their mother or father.

More than one in ten youngsters overall lives with cohabiting parents.

According to the definition of dependent children used by the Office for National Statistics – those under 16 or under 18 and still in full-

### By Steve Doughty, Social Affairs Correspondent

time education – there are 1,278,455 youngsters with unmarried, co-habiting parents among the total of 11,665,266.

Some 65 per cent of them live with their birth mother and father.

*Apart from children living with one parent, many more have seen their natural parents break up and now live with a stepfather or stepmother*

The statistics on social trends in family life were part of the third batch of data to be released from the 2001 Census.

Last November, the first results from the £200 million survey put the UK population at 58,789,194 on Census day.

It also highlighted Britain's ageing population as those over 60 outnumbered under-16s for the first time.

A further tranche of data issues in February gave more insight into ethnicity, religion, health, marriage and housing.

There are 21,660,475 households in England and Wales, of which 30 per cent (6.5 million) are occupied by one person – up from 26 per cent in 1991.

The Census findings are being released in stages because of the time taken to process the 20-page form everybody in the country was required to fill in. The demanding nature of the form was said, however, to have contributed to low returns – especially in inner-city areas – which have led to concerns over the accuracy of the result.

For instance, the first Census results showed the overall population to be one million less than was thought.

Officials said large numbers of people leaving the country had gone uncounted, among them 'young people clubbing in Ibiza'.

© *The Daily Mail*
*May 2003*

# Lone parents in the UK

## Information from Oxfam

*We commonly make the assumption that working for gender equality means working with women. The One Parent Families' Support and Information Network in the UK found that it was discriminating against men, and took action to address this. Sue Smith explains why the UK Poverty Programme is using this partner as a model to show other anti-poverty organisations in Britain how gender mainstreaming can be achieved.*

Twenty-two per cent of UK families are headed by a single parent and 90 per cent of lone parents are women. Lone parenthood no longer carries a heavy social stigma, but single parents face special problems such as access to affordable child-care facilities and flexible working hours. The need to work around school hours and holidays means that only part-time employment is open to them, which is usually low paid and low skilled. Lone fathers face additional problems of isolation and inappropriate services, as most child welfare services are framed around women's needs and life patterns.

The One Parent Families' Support and Information Network (YOPF) provides services to 3,000 lone parents in and around the city of York, in the north of England. The services include a drop-in centre, counselling and information, a range of courses, a toy library, and a second-hand clothes store. The organisation has had a proactive equal opportunities policy for several years and has developed transparent and accountable procedures on the recruitment, retention, and development of staff, and on reporting grievances.

It has constantly asked itself whether it is managing to include parents with disabilities, parents from ethnic minority groups, men and women, and gay and lesbian parents in its services.

### Asking for advice and support

The organisation approached Oxfam four years ago and has been supported through a series of grants, and ongoing advice on gender. Grants have been given for: outreach work to widen its contact with lone parents; a part-time worker to carry out a survey of who uses its services; and a series of workshops and research with lone fathers to look at how the organisation could meet their needs more effectively. The UKPP's gender adviser ran a workshop series on gender and parenting, gender and power, and gender and sexuality. The organisation has also acted as a pilot to test out Oxfam's 'gender impact toolkit', and has made recommendations on how to make it relevant to service-providing organisations.

YOPF's clear gender mainstreaming strategy has enabled it to make its services available to all lone parents, regardless of sex, race, or ability. It has collected gender-disaggregated information, done a clear gender analysis, and started to address the issue of gender relations being the source of poverty for children. It has changed its focus from service provision for individual lone parents to improving parenting skills, in order to address children's needs for support from both parents. While this has been achieved primarily through strong leadership and commitment, solid systems, and good organisation, Oxfam can claim some credit for making a broad range of support available to the organisation.

These were some of the steps along the way:

- The establishment of a resource centre resulted in an increase in the number of lone fathers coming to the centre for advice, support, and training.
- The gender mainstreaming strategy has successfully challenged the stereotypes that women are naturally better at caring than men, and that men are going to be worse at parenting.
- The organisation has changed its rules so that its services are equally available to lone fathers. Previously, the rules stated that a lone parent had to produce evidence of their status, such as the child benefit book (a state welfare benefit, almost always held by the mother), or evidence of a court order giving residency to the child (again, almost always given to the mother). Now they aim to 'promote the well-being of children by supporting the family as a whole where parents are sharing care on a regular basis'.
- It recognised that, in reality, lone parents are rarely 'lone' but that both parents share care of their children to some degree, and that the organisation should be focusing on ways to support better relations between the parents, in the long-term interests of the child.
- YOPF is developing a programme which focuses on better parenting relationships. The parenting course looks at how men and women parent differently and what each can learn from the other.

### Changing gender relations – to benefit everyone

As a result of all these efforts, gender relations have changed at a number of levels. In the drop-in centre, both men and women find the atmosphere more comfortable and open. Fewer

---

*Lone parenthood no longer carries a heavy social stigma, but single parents face special problems*

---

assumptions are made about the stereotypical roles of male and female parents, women feel less threatened and are more willing to overcome their initial suspicion, and men feel less judged and more welcomed. The first steps have been taken towards breaking down stereotypes in the use of services. More women are attending computer courses, and there has been an increase in the number of men using the counselling service.

A focus on the needs of children brought about a significant change in attitude among staff, through an understanding of how conflict and lack of co-operation between parents has an impact on children both now and in the future. Relations among staff have improved – both women and the one male worker have become more confident in raising issues and concerns as they come up. Female and male volunteers are more aware of the problems that the opposite sex may be facing – and in particular the need for privacy for men coming into an all-women space.

*By Sue Smith, Gender Adviser, Oxfam GB UK Poverty Programme*

- The above information is from Oxfam's web site which can be found at www.oxfam.org.uk

© Oxfam

## One-parent families in Scotland

### Key facts about one-parent families

- There are over 162,000 lone parents in Scotland, 93% of whom are women, with around 280,000 children. One-parent families are 25% of all families with dependent children.[1]
- 57% of lone parents have been married and are lone parents because they are divorced [31%], separated [21%] or widowed [5%].[2]
- While single or 'never married' lone parents are 42% of all lone parents, the majority were previously cohabiting or in a stable relationship and would be better described as separated cohabitees. Only 15% or 1 in 7 lone mothers have never married or lived with their child's father.[3]
- In 2000, 43% of children were born to unmarried parents. The majority of these [83%] were jointly registered and of these, 74% gave the same address for both parents.[4]
- Less than 3% of all lone parents are aged under 20 years. The average age is 35 years.[5]
- More than 50% of lone-parent householders in Scotland fall below 60% of the average household income. This is at least double the rate of anyone else.[6]
- 62% of children in one-parent families are poor. Nearly half of all poor children live in one-parent families.[7]
- In Scotland over 93,000 lone parents claim Income Support. Of these, 15,000 are in receipt of a pensioner or disability premium and 40,600 [43%] have a child under 5 years old.[8]

*Notes*
1  Office for National Statistics 2000, *Social Trends 30*
2  ONS 2001, *Labour Force Survey*
3  Haskey in *Population Trends 91*, ONS 1998
4  General Register Office for Scotland, 2002
5  DSS Research Report 138, 2001
6  *Monitoring Poverty & Social Exclusion in Scotland*: Kenway et al, Nov 2002; Joseph Rowntree Foundation
7  DSS 2001, *Households Below Average Income*
8  Income Support Quarterly Statistical Enquiry, May 2002

© One Parent Families Scotland

# Myths about lone parents

## Myths about lone parents still exist, survey reveals

**M**ost people overestimate the proportion of lone parents who are teenagers, according to a recent survey carried out by the charity One Parent Families and the Royal Bank of Scotland Group. Almost half the survey respondents thought twenty per cent of lone parents were teenagers and over a fifth put the proportion as high as 40 per cent. In fact, only three per cent of lone parents are teenagers – the average age of a lone parent is 35.

The survey also reveals that 80 per cent of people overestimate the number of lone mothers who've never married or lived with their child's father. Just over a quarter of respondents think between 31 and 50 per cent of lone mothers have never married or lived with their child's father, and almost half think that between 16 and 30 per cent haven't married or lived with the father.

In fact only 15 per cent of lone mothers have never married or lived with the father of their child.

'It is clear from the survey that there is some way to go before we've banished the myth that lone parenthood is a lifestyle choice,' said Andy Keen Downs, Deputy Director of One Parent Families. 'Most lone parents have not chosen to be parenting alone, and are doing so because of a marriage or relationship breakdown.

'One-parent families now make up a quarter of all British families and it's time there was more recognition that lone parents are ordinary parents, most of whom are struggling to bring up their children on a single income.'

Stephanie Allison, Community Investment Manager with the Royal Bank of Scotland Group, which has a three-year £500,000 partnership with One Parent Families, said: 'Financial issues are an acute concern for many single-parent families. RBS group believes in financial inclusion and one-parent families are one of the groups most vulnerable to poverty.

Our support for One Parent Families through the free Lone Parent Helpline aims to prevent lone parents being one of the most financially excluded groups in the UK today by providing practical information and advice to them when they need it most.'

Despite the misconceptions about who lone parents are, there is a better understanding from the general public about how difficult it is to raise children alone. Most people surveyed think it would be extremely difficult or difficult most of the time (51 per cent). And over 42 per cent think balancing work and children is the hardest thing about being a lone parent.

### Other results:

- 54 per cent of respondents think that J. K. Rowling is the best celebrity role model for lone parents.
- Almost 30 per cent think that feeling lonely and isolated is the hardest thing about being a lone parent.
- 24 per cent think the hardest thing is surviving on a low

*'Lone parents are ordinary parents, most of whom are struggling to bring up their children on a single income'*

income. (52 per cent of calls to the Lone Parent Helpline from England and Wales, and 51 per cent from Scotland, are on financial issues and child support.)

### Notes

1. One Parent Families is the leading charity providing direct services to lone parents and their children. The charity runs a Freephone Lone Parent Helpline on 0800 018 5026 (Mon – Fri 9 am to 5 pm) and produces free booklets on every aspect of one-parent-family life, from benefits and tax to childcare and legal rights to holidays for single parent families. The Lone Parent Helpline was launched in 2002 by the charity's Ambassador J. K. Rowling.

2. Last year, the Royal Bank of Scotland Group spent £33.7 million on its community investment programme. As well as One Parent Families, it has joined forces with a number of organisations that make a real impact on social and financial inclusion and education. It is also committed to encouraging its staff to make a contribution to their community.

■ The above information is from the Royal Bank of Scotland Group's web site which can be found at www.rbs.co.uk

© The Royal Bank of Scotland Group

# Single-handed parents

## By Jill Curtis

Today the words 'single parent' and 'lone parent' receive a bad press. But what of the women and men who find themselves thrust – perhaps against their will – into this position? Some women do choose to be single mothers and to create a family on their own, but this is by no means the majority, and those who do make this choice still find themselves faced by single-parent issues.

As the UK is the divorce capital of Europe, and as more children find themselves living with one parent these need to be addressed. According to SPAN (Single Parent Action Network) 23% of all families with children are lone-parent families – which makes a total of 1.3 million single parents in Britain. Ginger-bread ( an organisation dedicated to helping single parents) tells us that nine out of ten lone parents are mothers. Of course, there are fathers in a similar position – but for the sake of clarity I shall speak of 'mothers' with a real acknowledgement to the men bringing up a child on their own.

In my research for my books on the family I heard again and again of the prejudice single parents can feel directed towards them, particularly hard when they are struggling to keep afloat.

Annie: 'After my divorce I moved house with my three children. A year on our neighbour told me that they had all been dismayed when they heard a single-parent family was moving into the street. "We all thought the kids would be tearaways, but they are so well mannered." I was told this with obvious surprise, and relief.'

There needs to be a groundswell of opinion to combat the damage done to families by such labels. In news reports earlier this year of an alleged rape of a nine-year-old girl by boys of her peer group in a primary school the media, without exception, drew attention to the number of children at the school who lived in a single-parent family. This reinforces the belief that all single-parent families are dysfunctional.

Gloria: 'I will not let us be called a single-parent family. My son has two parents – how could it be otherwise? Divorce doesn't change that.'

The responsibility of being a single parent, with daily decisions about bringing up a child, and often trying to balance a tight budget, is a daunting one. All the evidence gathered over the years about the importance of caring for a child – especially under the age of three – is too often disregarded when there is pressure on a mother to work outside the home. Since the young child's experience of early mothering has a lifelong impact on his ability to make future close relationships, society needs to be aware of the consequences for the next generation if this is not valued. Children need consistency of care, individual attention and prompt response to distress. Especially after a divorce – which at best means partial loss of a parent – the importance of the presence of the resident parent cannot be emphasised too strongly.

But becoming a parent on your own to care for children does require a complete rethink. To be faced by this after the heartbreak of a death, divorce or separation can mean that it takes great courage to hold on to the belief that you are a good parent, and can care for the children on your own. That you are, in fact, still a family.

Emma: 'At thirty-nine and after seven years of marriage I found myself a single parent. I didn't choose to be one and, would you believe, at first could only think I must find a new partner. It took two years and many tears for me to realise that mum, and dad and kids are not the only combination to make up a "family".'

In time each parent finds her own way of regrouping as a family. Some band together with another single parent – whilst others gather a 'new' family around them including neighbours and close friends.

Family, if luckily enough to have an extended one, are hopefully also there for some back-up. But so too, are some organisations, run by either volunteers or professionals, who can help with the practical and emotional fall out. No longer are one-parent families prepared to fade into the background; they have a right to be accepted by the community. Joining organisations such as SPAN, Families Need Fathers and Ginger-bread often helps to discover advice about finance, debts and sometimes even where to go for a holiday.

On balance, the message which came through to me was that a parent on his or her own does feel very vulnerable. Society does little to make room for a lone parent. The happiest men and women on their own seemed to be those who had reassembled the marital jigsaw into a fresh picture, and from them a positive attitude did shine through.

Julie: 'Don't forget to have fun. Coping alone with domestic chores and worrying about money can mean fun can go out of the window. Don't let it.'

Diana: 'My kids are big fans of Barney and he has a great song about families. What the song basically says is that, "family is people and a family is love". It doesn't matter what your family consists of, just that you love each other. It is a great song for our situation.'

■ The above information is from Jill Curtis' web site which can be found at www.family2000.org

> **'I will not let us be called a single-parent family. My son has two parents'**

# Lone parenthood – a male perspective

## Information from Gingerbread

*By Robert Clark*

Lone parents are parasites who suck off the state – or at least that was my uninformed and prejudiced perception, until six years ago, when I found myself very suddenly and most unexpectedly a lone-parent father of three children aged from six to 11. A marital breakdown put me in the daunting position of being responsible for every aspect of their little lives while trying to hold down a job serving Queen and country as a British soldier – this, all in addition to the emotional roller-coaster normally experienced with divorce.

The first thing that became apparent was that the two were not compatible, and although the Army was superb in the support it gave me, I eventually had to change career to a more family-friendly position at a much lower salary. I had been a soldier since the age of 16 – it had been my life, but all of a sudden my priorities changed and I knew by instinct where my duty now lay.

The second, and possibly more hurtful, was the (albeit un-intentional) prejudice I experienced in society as a male lone parent. My social life disappeared overnight, the CSA always assumed I was the absent parent whenever I enquired why it was taking so long to process my claim. I had great difficulty getting the child benefit transferred into my name, and it was made clear to me that the legal system would automatically favour their mother, should she wish to change her mind and fight for custody of the children.

> *Lone-parent fatherhood is not easy, and brings with it some unique obstacles to overcome, but I survived*

However, all was not lost. I decided the only option was survival and looked for support systems – I was told about Gingerbread, which was initially described to me as 'a sort of coffee morning where you look after each other's kids'. No chance! But I later read an article in a men's magazine about lone-parent fathers and plucked up courage to contact my local group; I haven't looked back since. In Ashford Gingerbread I found like-minded company, a variety of social activities I had never thought of trying before, and a mutual support system – above all, I felt valued again as a human being.

It took me about two years to get back on my feet properly, and I am now a better person for it. I have a bond with my children that I could never have achieved in 'normal' circumstances and have a far wider outlook on life than before. Lone-parent fatherhood is not easy, and brings with it some unique obstacles to overcome, but I survived. There is a bright light at the end of the tunnel, even if it does occasionally turn out to be the headlight of an oncoming train!

■ The above information is from *Ginger*, Gingerbread's publication for all lone-parent families, Summer 2003.

© Gingerbread

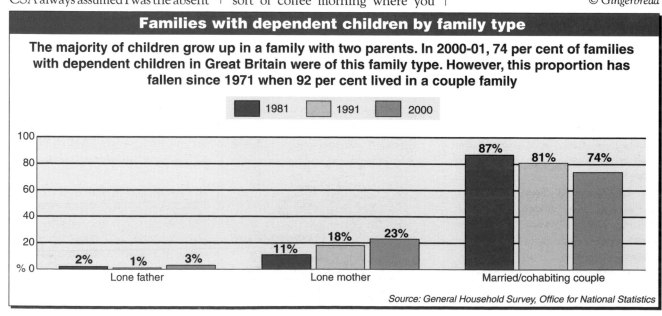

**Families with dependent children by family type**

The majority of children grow up in a family with two parents. In 2000-01, 74 per cent of families with dependent children in Great Britain were of this family type. However, this proportion has fallen since 1971 when 92 per cent lived in a couple family

Legend: ■ 1981 ■ 1991 ■ 2000

Lone father: 2%, 1%, 3%
Lone mother: 11%, 18%, 23%
Married/cohabiting couple: 87%, 81%, 74%

Source: General Household Survey, Office for National Statistics

# The other one-parent family

## Information from Fathers Direct

If we care about children today, we cannot escape the question of what happens to them when their parents split up. This is no longer a side issue: we know that before they are 16, one in eight children is living apart from at least one birth parent, typically their father. Such loss can have a big impact on a child. It also creates an important task for people working with families. This is to help muster all available resources to ensure the best possible outcome for these young people.

This edition of *FatherWork* has focused on what role fathers can play in this post-separation period. We don't have all the answers. This is a fraught subject, confused by the distress of broken relationships, the anger of men and women. But the most up-to-date research indicates that, in general, children do better after separation when they can maintain a relationship with mum *and* dad. The is the central finding of a new study, led by Judy Dunn, Research Professor in Psychology at the Institute of Psychiatry, King's College, London.

Professor Dunn also reports that a good relationship with dad is more likely when the estranged mother and father manage to maintain some sort of respectful relationship with each other.

Let us not just support one parent after family break-up, but give proper backing to both.

Setting aside their antagonism is also crucial for the child's general well-being: high levels of conflict, particularly when played out in court, damage the emotional health of children and boys, in particular, take a long time to recover. These conclusions also come from another impeccable source, the work of Dr Ann Buchanan from Oxford University's Department of Social Policy and Social Work.

How do we realise these principles? It would be easy, from the outset, to get bogged down in the rights and wrongs of the family court system. But that would be a mistake, since the vast majority of separating parents come to an arrangement without reference to the courts. So, for now, let's deal with the majority.

Up until now, we have tended to characterise these families as breaking up into 'one-parent families' led usually by mum, and a 'non-resident parent' usually the father. We have dispersed what meagre resources the state offers to the 'one-parent family' and largely ignored the 'non-resident father'.

---

### *Children do better after separation when they can maintain a relationship with mum and dad*

---

But if we accept that children thrive better when supported by both parents, this model does not work, since it fails to nurture and harness the potential of the non-resident parent. We believe it is time for the UK to use the analysis already adopted by One Parent Families, Scotland: namely that, after separation, two one-parent families

are created, one led by the mother and the other by the father.

Once this is done, one begins to realise how much children are being failed. Millions of them are spending substantial periods of time in one-parent families led by fathers, (so-called 'non-resident dads') who have poor accommodation, little training in childcare, scant financial support and minimal emotional support from services. We could make so much more of these dads if we valued their potential contribution properly.

The other task for family services is to offer support for parental relationships even when couples have divorced or separated. If the parents cannot get on then the research shows that dad is likely to lose his relationship with the children, which is bad news for the children. Not surprisingly, this is particularly true for teenage parents. It explains how 80 per cent of the children of teenage fathers are out of touch with dad by the time they are 15.

So it is time to chuck out the model of just supporting one parent and replace it with one that tries to create a working relationship even between estranged and embittered couples. It's an emotional minefield, tough work, but unavoidable.

We will deal with the family courts in another edition. But one message from up-to-date research is crystal clear. It is hard to imagine a setting worse than an adversarial legal system for putting families on the right footing after separation.

■ The above information is from *FatherWork* magazine, a quarterly journal for people working with families, published by Fathers Direct, the national information centre on fatherhood. It was published at Christmas 2002.

© *Fathers Direct*

# Saturday fatherhood

**The family lives of separated dads are often misunderstood, writes Andrew Purvis, father of Laurence, 14, and Rosie, 12,**

On trains, Tubes, buses and at motorway service stations you see us – thousands of ordinary family men, embarking every Sunday evening on a poignant one-way journey. The outward trip is a melée of hurled Ribena cartons, last-minute homework, toys, tears and treble voices. On the way back, there is only silence and a dull feeling of regret, as we focus on Monday morning, work and the childless week ahead. We may be known as 'absent fathers' – but on Sunday nights, it feels as if our children are absent from us.

A decade ago, when I entered this strange, bi-polar world of the non-custodial parent, I didn't like it one bit. When you've cradled their bloody heads after birth, stoically allowed them to be sick on you and fed them at 5am for weeks, it's hard to see your children as a weekend luxury. 'Forget the kids and begin a new life,' one family member advised, a few weeks after the split, but it seemed like advice from another century. Most of the men I knew were deeply involved with their children and some were more hands-on than their wives. It seemed unthinkable to abandon Laurence and Rosie, even when the rows about money and mortgages had eroded our goodwill and left me bankrupt. Somehow, a higher instinct kicked in – a desire to see my kids through to their teenage years and beyond, a need to mould them, guide them and keep them a product of both of us, not just the parent they lived with. It was the triumph of genetic code over postcode.

Almost immediately, we agreed a solution. Laurence and Rosie, who were four and two, would stay with me on alternate weekends and I'd drop by during the week as well. In those early days, their chattering presence illuminated my dark world. They were always good company; they were never petty. Somehow, they were unwaveringly loyal to me and to their mother. Of course there were some hair-raising moments – a plane journey to Spain, my first as a single parent, when they needed the toilet 17 times. The time Laurence 'walked' his pushchair off the kerb and cracked his head on a parked Volvo. These are things we talk about now, our shared history of narrowly-avoided disaster.

---

*When you've cradled their bloody heads after birth, stoically allowed them to be sick on you and fed them at 5am for weeks, it's hard to see your children as a weekend luxury*

---

Over the years, I have come to realise that being a weekend father carries little stigma. It may not be an ideal scenario – but it is less a failure, more a different, experimental way of living. My children feel loved in two households, not one; they have their possessions scattered throughout both. My new partner and I attend school plays and carol concerts and sit in the same pew as my ex-wife and her new partner. Afterwards, we all go for a drink – and the kids love it.

The stereotype of the weekend father as a sad, remote, emotionally inarticulate stranger passing a few hours with his kids in parks and burger restaurants may be accurate in a few cases, but it doesn't match my experience. Nor does the American idea of the 'Disneyland Dad' – a man who ruins his kids with expensive treats. From the outset, I couldn't afford it. These days, the world of the weekend father is a world of homework, PlayStations, frank conversation and lazy Saturday mornings at home – not that of the frenetic Redcoat or the tragicomic clown. It is just a different kind of normality.

■ The above information is from *FatherWork* magazine, a quarterly journal for people working with families, published by Fathers Direct, the national information centre on fatherhood. It was published at Christmas 2002.

© Fathers Direct

# Swinging it as a single

## Jill Insley on how to survive the financial perils of being a lone parent

Children are expensive enough when there are two parents to meet the costs, but for a single parent the burden can prove overwhelming.

'I had a pretty rough night last night,' says a correspondent logged on to the chatroom run by Gingerbread, a charitable information service for single parents. 'Nothing particularly bad, but living on income support and paying 30% of your benefits every month just to pay off debts my ex has saddled me with does get me down. It's really hard to sleep at night with £7,000 worth of debts, so I only got about an hour or two's sleep between the panic attacks.'

The Government attempted to improve the finances of the 1.7 million single-parent families through a raft of measures in its 1997 'family-first' Budget, including the New Deal for Lone Parents, a one-to-one support scheme that aims to help people back into work. But five years on, many of those who are in work believe they are little better off than those on state benefits.

Jo Casebourne, of the Centre for Social and Economic Inclusion, says the main reason for this has been that many single parents start at the bottom of the work ladder, in part-time or temporary jobs with few employee benefits and no security. 'They are likely to earn a little bit more than they would have received in employee benefits – about £20 or so – but this can easily be wiped out by work-related expenses,' she said.

Although the Government revamped the New Deal scheme to enable people to apply for more skilled jobs, even single parents earning decent salaries struggle to come to terms with living on one income. Jane earns more than £50,000 a year, but has built up a frightening level of debt since her divorce nearly three years ago. 'I know I earn a good salary and my ex pays generous maintenance, but I

still don't seem able to make ends meet,' she says. 'I've got credit cards, a loan and an overdraft, and every month I seem to be further in debt.'

The Consumer Credit Counselling Service says it is common for people to end up in debt at the end of a relationship. Geeta Varma, a counsellor with the service, says: 'Sometimes debt problems are the cause of the relationship breaking up, sometimes the debts build up because of the break-up.'

---

*'Sometimes debt problems are the cause of the relationship breaking up, sometimes the debts build up because of the break-up'*

---

Parents often make the mistake of trying to continue living exactly as they did before, even though their financial circumstances have changed. 'There's this attitude of "the children mustn't suffer". People often live beyond their means. It's difficult for them to realise that if their finances have changed, their lifestyle must change too.'

Although all our case studies are women, Varma says men often end up in debt as well, even if they do not have custody of the children. 'It costs a lot to set up home in the first place, and if the man is the bigger earner, many if not all of the credit agreements will be set up in his name. Then if he moves out when the relationship finishes, he will be left paying off the debts while she keeps the goods.'

### 'I am not much better off in a full-time job'

'I separated from my husband last year. He left me with all the bills from our marriage and no money. I was working at the time, but as we were at the same company I had to give up work and start elsewhere.

'I find every month a continual struggle to meet all bills and the high cost of rented accommodation – it's often a juggling act of who is screaming the loudest [for money]. My ex only pays towards our daughter because the Child Support Agency finally managed to sort it all out, although there is back pay still outstanding and it doesn't go back to when he first left, only to when he first completed the forms sent to him.

'I have tried to get alternative accommodation by registering with councils and housing associations but as they deem me to be properly housed (not that they'd live in a place like this or for this much money!), I stand no hope of getting social housing. Although the amount I pay for rent would more than cover a mortgage, I cannot get a mortgage as I don't earn enough for their sums.

'Childcare is another issue. During term time, my daughter attends the school club, but in the holidays she goes somewhere different and the cost doubles. I get no help towards that either.

'I am not much better off working full time than I would be living off benefits – probably about £20 per week better off, but it gets me out of the house and gives me a chance to socialise and keep sane.'

### 'I get no contribution from the ex. He is on sickness benefit'

'Since [my partner] left in January my finances have improved, inasmuch as he isn't bleeding us dry any more. I've been able to take out important things like insurance and a pension to safeguard our future.

'I work full-time and get disabled person's tax credit [DTC] at the moment, but would probably be better off not working. I carry on with my job because it is important from the social side.

'The things that are difficult are the fact that my combined income – wage and DTC – take me outside the housing benefit threshold, so I get no assistance with rent or council tax [£385 per month total out of an income of £1,000].

'In addition, DTC doesn't get you help with school dinners [£25 a week] or school clothing, and all three of my children need to have school uniforms.

---

## 'I am not much better ]off working full time than I would be living off benefits – probably about £20 per week better off'

'I budget carefully to enable us to have a holiday, presents and birthday parties. I'd like to have more of a social life but it isn't possible financially.

'I am fortunate that the eldest is old enough to babysit for me (I pay him but not what a "regular" baby-sitter would cost).

'My mum helps with the child-care, although I employ a child-minder for two hours a week at a cost of £15 for two of the children – but

the bulk of this is offset [£13.14] against my DTC, so I am no worse off there.

'I get no contributions from the ex – he is on sickness benefit and gets his rent and council tax paid for him, but (he says) he can't afford even minimal contributions.'

### 'There's no incentive to work hard'

'I will have been divorced for two years in December. My ex built up a lot of debt when we were together – and afterwards.

'After our divorce he declared himself bankrupt and has now been sacked for misuse of a company credit card. This means that, because he had not instructed a solicitor to sort out the financial side of our divorce and I was still battling to get the house transferred into my name, the trustees are forcing me to sell our property to pay off his debts – most of which were accumulated after our separation. Because he has been sacked, he doesn't pay maintenance.

'I work full time, maintain three children and run a house, which is a massive struggle. I get working tax credit, so do not qualify for any other benefits, not even free school meals.

'If I worked only 16 hours a week, I would be entitled to everything – there is no real incentive to work full-time.'

■ This article first appeared in *The Observer*, September 2002.

# Challenges for a better future

## Information from One Parent Families

Today, lone parents head one-quarter of all families in Britain. Nearly everyone knows and cares about someone in this situation. Every lone parent has their own life, their own personal history – they don't all share the same experiences. But they do share one thing – the experience of public prejudice and of being portrayed as just a 'burden on the state'. All political parties now agree it is wrong to portray lone parents in this way. We want their help to make change happen.

Most lone parents do not choose to be a parent on their own; none chooses to be poor. But over time, policies have institutionalised poverty in one-parent families. It is time to right this injustice – no one in a one-parent family should have to wait any longer for progress. Help us to make change happen today.

### Becoming a lone parent

- Parents need constructive mediation, advice and support to help reduce disputes during divorce and separation, and to protect the best interests and financial security of their children.
- Lone parents are vulnerable to poverty and isolation. Incomes typically fall significantly after divorce or separation – after all, there is only one income to protect children from poverty and one person both to earn and care for children.
- One-parent families need positive support, not stigmatising – child maintenance, access to decent

*Most lone parents do not choose to be a parent on their own; none chooses to be poor*

**One parent families**
making change happen

housing, help setting up a new home, childcare and financial support are all essential.
*Challenge: End poverty in one-parent families.*

### Looking after children

- Children are expensive – parents need help in meeting these costs.
- Children need to be kept safe and warm. New mothers and babies need adequate incomes, and an adequate diet, to ensure they are fit and healthy and able to take on new responsibilities and consider a return to work.
- Children of lone parents may need their parents to be at home to care for them for a while. Parents need the financial support to enable them to do this.
- Parents know what is best for their children, and need to be supported in the choices they make about work and childcare.
*Challenge: Give all children an equal start in life.*

### Starting work

- In order to get and keep paid work lone parents need a suitable job, an adequate income, acceptable childcare and knowledge and confidence about how to get a job and manage the competing demands of paid work and parenting. They need stability and security in all these areas but also in personal relationships, health and housing circumstances.
- Significant barriers to work, train and study remain, such as lack of childcare and high housing costs. These barriers must be removed.

- Unequal and low pay must continue to be addressed and more help is needed to make work pay – particularly for lone parents working part time.
- Children need to be looked after and lone parents have only one pair of hands – the new family-friendly rights at work must be built on and paid parental leave is essential.
*Challenge: Remove existing barriers to education, training and better-paid work.*

*One-parent families need positive support, not stigmatising*

### Looking to the future

- Lone parenthood is usually a temporary stage in the family lifecycle, lasting on average for five-and-a-half years.
- However, many lone parents face an uncertain future and poverty in old age due to the sacrifices they make as lone parents as their children grow up.
- More help is needed to help lone parents to qualify for contributory benefits and pensions, and to prevent them from paying a lifelong forfeit for parenthood and gender through low or lost earnings.
*Challenge: Think long term and ensure that lone parents achieve security in old age.*

■ The above information is from One Parent Families' 2003 Manifesto *Making Change Happen*. For more information visit their web site which can be found at www.oneparentfamilies.org.uk
© One Parent Families

# KEY FACTS

- The UK has the highest rate of teenage pregnancies in western Europe. (p. 01)

- All young people must have access to services that will provide information about sexual health and a range of contraceptive choices. (p. 02)

- Teenagers are far less likely to get pregnant today than they were in the early 1970s. The conception rate in 1970 was 82.4 per 1,000 15- 19-year-olds compared with 60.9 in 2001. (p. 04)

- The teenage conception rate is considerably higher in deprived areas of the country compared with affluent areas. (p. 05)

- 'Teenage mothers are amongst the poorest and most vulnerable people in the UK'. (p. 10)

- 'Young people sometimes do make the choice to have a child. No one wants to deny them that right'. (p. 11)

- Society often views young fathers in a negative light. This leads them to feel undervalued, disregarded and excluded and this can lead them to withdraw from family life, losing their self-esteem, and can have a serious effect on their confidence. (p. 12)

- 'People should know there are other measures such as the "morning-after" pill. The government should take action and have an advertising campaign to spread the word.' (p. 13)

- The UK has one of the highest teenage pregnancy rates in the developed world, with 31 births per 1,000 girls aged between 15 and 19 in 1998 although the rate has been falling. (p. 14)

- A quarter (25 per cent) of women interviewed were not using any method of contraception, and half of these women (13 per cent of all women aged 16-49) were not currently in a heterosexual relationship. (p. 15)

- Britain is the teenage pregnancy capital of Europe; abortion is at an all-time high and we are in the grip of a huge epidemic of sexually transmitted infections which is threatening the fertility of the next generation. (p. 17)

- Sex education seeks to reduce the risks of potentially negative outcomes from sexual behaviour. (p. 21)

- Boys and young men are 'half the solution' to reducing pregnancies and more needed to be done to get them involved in 'sex and relationship education' in school. (p. 23)

- Parents also have the right to withdraw their children from sex education lessons they feel inappropriate. (p. 24)

- In 2001, conception rates in under-18s were 3% lower than in 2000. The total reduction since 1998 is 9% which means that around 8,000 pregnancies in girls under 18 have been pre-vented. Conception rates in under-16s in 2001 were 4.5% lower than in 2000, with an overall reduction of over 10% since 1998. (p. 25)

- Teenagers are being taught that not only is abstinence the morally correct path to take, but that it is also the only certain method of preventing STIs and pregnancy. (p. 26)

- It may seem unnecessary to define a 'lone' parent. For official purposes, however, a lone-parent family is one where: 'A mother or father living without a spouse (and not co-habiting) with his or her never-married dependent child or children aged either under 16 or from 16 to 19 and undertaking full-time education.' (p. 28)

- Twenty-two per cent of UK families are headed by a single parent and 90 per cent of lone parents are women. Lone parenthood no longer carries a heavy social stigma, but single parents face special problems such as access to affordable child-care facilities and flexible working hours. (p. 3p. 3)

- 'Lone parents are ordinary parents, most of whom are struggling to bring up their children on a single income'. (p. 32)

- Children do better after separation when they can maintain a relationship with mum and dad. (p. 35)

- The Government attempted to improve the finances of the 1.7 million single-parent families through a raft of measures in its 1997 'family-first' Budget, including the New Deal for Lone Parents, a one-to-one support scheme that aims to help people back into work. But five years on, many of those who are in work believe they are little better off than those on state benefits. (p. 37)

- Single parents start at the bottom of the work ladder, in part-time or temporary jobs with few employee benefits and no security. 'They are likely to earn a little bit more than they would have received in employee benefits – about £20 or so – but this can easily be wiped out by work-related expenses'. (p. 37)

- Most lone parents do not choose to be a parent on their own; none chooses to be poor. (p. 39)

- One-parent families need positive support, not stigmatising. (p. 39)

# ADDITIONAL RESOURCES

You might like to contact the following organisations for further information. Due to the increasing cost of postage, many organisations cannot respond to enquiries unless they receive a stamped, addressed envelope.

**AVERT**
4 Brighton Road
Horsham
West Sussex, RH13 5BA
Tel: 01403 210202
Fax: 01403 211001
avert@dial.pipex.com
Web site: www.avert.org
AVERT is a leading UK AIDS Education and Medical Research charity. They are responsible for a wide range of education and medical research work.

**Barnardo's**
Tanners Lane
Barkingside
Ilford, Essex, IG6 1QG
Tel: 020 8550 8822
Fax: 020 8551 6870
E-mail:
media.team@barnardos.org.uk
Web site: www.barnardos.org.uk
Barnardo's works with over 47,000 children, young people and their families in more than 300 projects across the county.

**Brook**
Unit 421, Highgate Studios
53-79 Highgate Road
London, NW5 1TL
Tel: 020 7284 6040
Fax: 020 7284 6050
E-mail: admin@brookcentres.org.uk
Web site: www.brook.org.uk
Brook is the only national voluntary sector provider of free and confidential sexual health advice and services specifically for young people under 25.

**Fathers Direct**
Herald House
15 Lamb's Passage
Bunhill Row
London, EC1Y 8TQ
Tel: 020 7920 9491
Fax: 020 7374 2966
E-mail: mail@fathersdirect.com
Web site: www.fathersdirect.com
Fathers Direct is the national information centre for fatherhood. They work to ensure that children, particularly socially deprived children, get the best possible love and care from their fathers.

**fpa (formerly The Family Planning Association)**
2-12 Pentonville Road
London, N1 9FP
Tel: 020 7837 5432
Fax: 020 7837 3042
Web site: www.fpa.org.uk
Produces information and publications on all aspects of reproduction and sexual health – phone for a publications catalogue. The Helpline on 020 7837 4044 Monday-Friday 9am to 7pm is run by qualified healthcare workers and can answer queries on all aspects of family planning.

**Gingerbread**
7 Sovereign Court
Sovereign Close
London, E1W 3HW
Tel: 020 7488 9300
Fax: 020 7488 9333
office@gingerbread.org.uk
Web site: www.gingerbread.org.uk
Gingerbread is the leading support organisation for lone-parent families in England and Wales. Helpline: 0800 018 4318. Open 10am to 4pm Monday to Friday.

**Health Development Agency**
Holborn Gate
330 High Holborn
London, WC1V 7BA
Tel: 020 7430 0850
Fax: 020 7061 3390
E-mail: communications@hda-online.org.uk
Web site: www.hda.nhs.uk
The Health Development Agency (HDA) identifies the evidence of what works to improve people's health and reduce health inequalities.

**International Planned Parenthood Federation (IPPF)**
Regent's College
Inner Circle, Regent's Park
London, NW1 4NS
Tel: 020 7487 7900
Fax: 020 7487 7950
E-mail: info@ippf.org
Web site: www.ippf.org
The largest voluntary organisation in the field of sexual and reproductive health including family planning, represented in over 180 countries worldwide.

**One Parent Families (OPF)**
255 Kentish Town Road
London, NW5 2LX
Tel: 020 7428 5400
Fax: 020 7482 4851
E-mail:
info@oneparentfamilies.org.uk
Web site:
www.oneparentfamilies.org.uk
One Parent Families promotes the welfare of lone parents and their children. Their aim is to overcome the poverty, isolation and social exclusion which so many face.

**One Parent Families Scotland**
13 Gayfield Square
Edinburgh, EH1 3NX
Tel: 0131 556 3899 / 4563
Fax: 0131 557 9650
E-mail: info@opfs.org.uk
Web site: www.opfs.org.uk

**Oxfam**
Oxfam House, 274 Banbury Road
Oxford, OX2 7DZ
Tel: 01865 311311
Fax: 01865 312600
E-mail: oxfam@oxfam.org.uk
Web site: www.oxfam.org.uk
Oxfam is a development, relief, and campaigning organisation dedicated to finding lasting solutions to poverty and suffering around the world.

**YWCA**
Clarendon House
52 Cornmarket Street
Oxford, OX1 3EJ
Tel: 01865 304200
Fax: 01865 204805
E-mail: info@ywca-gb.org.uk
Web site: www.ywca-gb.org.uk
The YWCA in England and Wales is a force for change for women who are facing discrimination and inequalities of all kinds.

# INDEX

# ACKNOWLEDGEMENTS

The publisher is grateful for permission to reproduce the following material.

While every care has been taken to trace and acknowledge copyright, the publisher tenders its apology for any accidental infringement or where copyright has proved untraceable. The publisher would be pleased to come to a suitable arrangement in any such case with the rightful owner.

### Chapter One: Teenage Parents

*Teenage pregnancy and parenthood*, © Health Development Agency 2003, *Teenage pregnancy*, © fpa, *Teenage conception rates down*, © Crown copyright is reproduced with the permission of Her Majesty's Stationery Office, *Teenage conceptions*, © Brook, *Junior jury: teen pregnancy*, © Children's Express, *'People are constantly judging us'*, © Thomas Vipond, *The problems of parenthood*, © Barnardo's, *Teenage pregnancy*, © youthinformation.com, *Current use of contraception*, © Crown copyright is reproduced with the permission of Her Majesty's Stationery Office, *Poverty and young motherhood* © YWCA, *Supporting young mums*, © Health Development Agency 2003, *Young fathers*, © youthinformation.com, *British teenagers talk*, © International Planned Parenthood Federation (IPPF), *The teenage girls whose 'career' choice is pregnancy*, © The Daily Mail, October 2003, *Contraception and sexual health*, © Crown copyright is reproduced with the permission of Her Majesty's Stationery Office, *The teenage sex epidemic*, © The Daily Mail, October 2003, *Source of information about STIs*, © Crown copyright is reproduced with the permission of Her Majesty's Stationery Office, *Explicit sex lessons fail to cut teen pregnancies*, © Telegraph Group Limited, London 2003, *Sex education that works*, © AVERT, *Cut benefits for mothers in teens, says family group*, © Telegraph Group Limited, London 2003, *'Tackle boys to tackle teen pregnancies'*, © The Daily Mail, July 2003, *Juniors' sex education 'should be compulsory'*, © Telegraph Group Limited, London 2003, *Teenage conception rates down*, © Crown copyright is reproduced with the permission of Her Majesty's Stationery Office, *Is abstinence the answer?*, © The Daily Mail, October 2003.

### Chapter Two: Lone-Parent Families

*Some facts and figures*, © The Skills and Learning Intelligence Module (SLIM), *Lone parents*, © Crown copyright is reproduced with the permission of Her Majesty's Stationery Office, *One child in four is being raised by a single parent*, © The Daily Mail, May 2003, *Lone parents in the UK*, © Oxfam, *One parent families in Scotland*, © One Parent Families Scotland, *Myths about lone parents*, © Royal Bank of Scotland Group, *Single-handed parents*, © Jill Curtis, *Lone parenthood – a male perspective*, © Gingerbread, *Families with dependent children by family type*, © Crown copyright is reproduced with the permission of Her Majesty's Stationery Office, *The other one parent family*, © Fathers Direct, *Saturday fatherhood*, © Fathers Direct, *Swinging it as a single*, © Guardian Newspapers Limited 2003, *Challenges for a better future*, © One Parent Families.

### Photographs and illustrations:

Pages 1, 15, 25, 30, 32, 38: Simon Kneebone; pages 5, 23, 36: Pumpkin House, pages 7, 16, 29, 37: Bev Aisbett.

Craig Donnellan
Cambridge
January, 2004